Creative
DRAMA

IN RELIGIOUS EDUCATION

Creative DRAMA

IN RELIGIOUS EDUCATION

by

ISABEL B. BURGER

Illustrations by Joyce Dillenberger

Morehouse-Barlow Co., Inc.
Wilton, Connecticut

Copyright © 1977 Morehouse-Barlow Company, Inc.
78 Danbury Road, Wilton, Connecticut 06897
SBN: 0-8192-1223-7
Library of Congress Card No. 77-70797

Printed in the United States of America

THIS BOOK IS LOVINGLY DEDICATED TO

*All the children who have
filled my classes and my life with
joy, especially my own children
and grandchildren, whose beautiful
thoughts have inspired this work*

Foreword

The creative drama class was over. The boys and girls had to be reminded that the clock on the Green Room wall said 5:40. Despite the fact that they were already ten minutes late, the children were loath to leave. Nobody even noticed that it was dark outside. I was so busy hurrying them off to meet impatient parents that, for the moment, I forgot that we had a very important guest observer. As I turned back into the room to put things in order, she faced me — the new Director of Religious Education for the Episcopal Diocese. I seldom blush, but I was well aware of burning cheeks as I took both her hands in apology. "Forgive me . . . forgive *us*, my dear! We were so deeply involved in that last exercise that I fear we were unintentionally very rude. We forgot that we even had a guest. I *am* sorry!"

She was so kind, her gentle smile full of understanding! I hurried on, still embarrassed: "Well, what do you think of our creative drama project? Has it any meaning for you and your work here?" There was a moment of silence. Then, her eyes shining, she squeezed my hands that she still held in hers. Finally, she spoke with quiet excitement: "This may be a creative drama class, but what I have experienced this afternoon is a miraculous example of religious education in a vital, effective, unusual form. I'm grateful!"

I was too touched to reply. Suddenly, these few words not only made the labor of twenty years worthwhile but challenged me to double my efforts for the next twenty. I firmly believe that it was these words, echoing in my heart for so long, that have made the following pages possible. They contain philosophies, techniques and materials which were developed because of thoughts spoken by a lady of strong faith, greatness of spirit, and depth in human understanding. She reinforced what my heart had been telling me for many years — that in the creative drama experience, skillfully directed, one has an unequaled instrument for the effective development of the Christian personality.

I sincerely hope that some of the suggestions and information included will assist the capable leaders already working in this field. If it inspires newcomers with confidence to try the techniques, I can promise them an exciting and rewarding experience.

Isabel B. Burger

Acknowledgments

To express my thanks to all who have given me inspiration, assistance, and suggestions for this book would take another volume. I must limit myself to just a few expressions of gratitude, knowing that I am likely to make some important omissions.

Much of the material, especially in the section devoted to the plays, came from hundreds of young people with whom I have worked in church school classes, conferences and special workshops, both here and abroad. They are the real authors; they have earned the readers' gratitude and mine.

To the Ronald Press Company in New York, publishers of the revised edition of my textbook, *Creative Play Acting*, (© 1966), I owe the greatest debt. They have graciously permitted me to draw heavily upon the sections in that book dealing with the practical procedures essential to any creative drama project. These were explained in great detail in *Creative Play Acting*, and since the step-by-step method is similar for secular and religious purposes, it seemed logical to draw some of this information from the original source. I am very thankful to the editors at Ronald Press for saving me so much time and effort.

The support and encouragement of my old friend Emma Twiggs, formerly Director of Religious Education for the Episcopal Diocese of Maryland, has deepened my understanding and motivated my further experimentation in this field for many years.

Many thoughts of gratitude also go to the Maryvale School, in Brooklandville, Maryland, where, under the inspiring guidance of the Sisters of Notre Dame de Namur, I was able to experiment with creative drama at the high school level for twelve years. We had unusual success in developing sensitivity, responsiveness and human understanding in the students. Special thanks to Sister Regina, S.N.D., former Principal of Maryvale and currently in the same position at the Academy of Notre Dame, in Villanova, Pennsylvania who wrote me a wonderfully encouraging letter when she heard of my plans to write this book. I am deeply grateful for the trust and esteem of such an eminent Christian educator.

The Right Reverend Richard Baker, retired Episcopal Bishop of North Carolina and my rector at the Church of the Redeemer in Baltimore for many years, gave me constant encouragement and dozens of opportunities to utilize creative drama methods in the church school. Bishop Baker's encouragement over the years and his continuing support are very precious to me.

To the many good friends and teachers who have been consulting with me on this manuscript and have generously provided ideas and assistance, especially Stacy Marckwald and Celeste Bobbett, I give my hearty thanks. Their guidance has been invaluable.

The research papers and published works of my many colleagues and fellow workers in the American Theatre Association, as well as studies of specialists abroad, have been extremely helpful in gathering comparative, as well as supportive material for this volume.

Special thanks are due to Pam Woody of Los Angeles, Chairman of the Religious Drama Committee of the National Children's Theatre Association of the American Theatre Association. Her recently compiled bibliography on "Creative Dramatics as a Subject or Method in Religious Education" has provided much of the comprehensive listing of supplementary material which appears on the last pages of this book.

Finally, I am grateful to the editorial staff of Morehouse-Barlow, publishers. They have been long-suffering and patient with my unavoidable delays; only their expertise in handling much of the technical detail and arranging for the delightful illustrations of Joyce Dillenberger made it possible to meet our publishing deadline. As a new author on their list, I want to express my sincere gratitude.

Contents

1

Christian Living
In A Troubled World

There is no denying the fact that the world we live in is a complex and troubled one. We are part of an uncomfortable, disturbed, and restless society composed of far too many cynical and disillusioned people, who find it difficult ever to catch a gleam of light or hope at the end of future's tunnel. One can understand their despair, but not willingly join their ranks. A well-known journalist wrote from Paris, just after Robert Kennedy's assassination: " . . . the entire world is seething with cultural revolutions, rioting and unrest, transcending ideological frontiers." At the same time another commentator said: "Mankind itself is ill, wherever he dwells . . . man around the world is absent from his brother's glory, abstaining from the comforting hand upon his shoulder. Hate and avarice stand like poised vultures in the thoughts of men . . . ."

These and other writers paint a gloomy picture of the world in which we are trying to function. We must be thankful, therefore, for other great leaders who offer a more affirmative and sustaining philosophy. Dr. John Krantz, formerly at the University of Maryland's Medical School is one of these. He said once to his graduating class: " . . . one cannot be a good physician unless he is a *good man*." He went on to discuss the attributes of a *good man*. "First, he embraces the triangle of faith — faith in God, faith in his fellow man, and faith in himself. The faith of the GOOD MAN dispels the fleecelike fog of anxiety which has enveloped a segment of the younger generation. What this world needs desperately are men and women with the eternal goodness of a Golden Rule in their hearts, to match the scientific and medical greatness of the hour in which we are privileged to live."

It is a great hour, and it is time, now, today, for us to work seriously on becoming good men and women and to bend every effort to help others to become caring, concerned, involved Christians. I remember a touching story, almost a parable, which my own pastor used many years ago to reply to a query put to him by a group of parishioners. They asked, "What kind of people would you like to see your church family become, if they are to work with you to create a strong Christian parish?" This story was his reply: "A little boy named Sam, an absent-minded but delightfully imaginative little fellow, had a hard time paying strict attention to his church school teacher. One bright day in October, the class was meeting as usual, in the little country church before the regular service. The teacher, in preparation for the festival at the end of the month, was discussing saints and their attributes. Finally, as she saw Sam's eyes wandering again, she stopped abruptly, determined to bring his mind back to the subject at hand. 'Sam,' she asked, a bit sternly, 'perhaps you can tell us what a saint is?' Sam came back to the real world with an uncomfortable bump. Then, suddenly, his eyes were caught by the sun streaming through the stained glass window behind the altar. He thought for a moment and then spoke with conviction: 'Miss Thomas, a saint is somebody the light shines through!' There was a moment of silence; all eyes turned toward the jewelled sunlight. Finally Miss Thomas spoke, 'That's right, Sam. A saint is surely someone through whom the light of God's love shines.' " "So," our pastor added, "what I wish for most is a parish where each of us works to become a small saint — a good person — the kind through whom the light of God's love shines!"

Where do we find the prescription? How do we go about helping one another to become happy, small saints? As we try to answer this question, we will examine the dramatic experience as a facilitator of this kind of growth.

First, we cannot gain happiness or goodness by becoming absorbed in the vehement pursuit of it. Reuel Howe says: "Preoccupation with one's own moral state or emotional life is self-destroying. Jesus taught men not to look in on themselves, but to the other, whether man or God; to love, to give, to affirm, to forgive." Nor can we sit in isolation waiting for happiness to find us. It is not an "alone" affair; it depends entirely on relationships and involvements with God, with one's fellow man, and with one's self. The more one concentrates on his own desires, success and ambitions, the less goodness and joy will come his way. Yet, paradoxically, three-fourths of the daily thoughts of the average person are centered on the self — pride in personal talents or material gains, self-pity because he feels that his lot is unduly hard, or hatred of the ineffectual self who cannot keep in step with his neighbors. These self chains drag him down, set him apart from his brothers, making impossible the building of close relationships upon which true happiness and goodness depend. Martin Buber in *I and Thou* speaks to this point when he says: "A person makes his appearance by entering into relationship with other persons."

A person is first faced with the need for keeping the lines of communication open by eliminating these self-centered thoughts which bind him. Once this is accomplished, he can enter into a healthy, two-way communication, a giving and receiving of love, kindness, human sympathy, compassion. As we give love and understanding, we receive in good measure; as we sensitively respond to the thoughts and feelings of another, our own thoughts and feelings are revived and extended. It is through this interplay of values, which has been called "creative interaction" that one is enriched so that he can stretch his spiritual wings.

To be able to give, to communicate thought and feeling to others freely, one must keep his "sending apparatus" in good repair. The message should reach its destination with the feeling and the meaning intended. How often has a friend been heard to say: "Well, you don't sound as though you care at all!" And the reply is inevitable: "But of course I care! Didn't I say so?" Unfortunately, something happened to the meaning of the communication; the words were there but completely unconvincing because they had no heart. The diagnosis is simple. One communicates with the *whole* self — body, mind, and spirit. If a single part is not functioning, the communication becomes ineffective and meaningless. The therapy, then, must be the providing of experiences which will offer simultaneous exercise of the whole self — body, mind, and spirit. Secondly, these experiences must serve to eliminate an unhealthy concentration on self.

It is only when a person has accepted himself for what he is, promising to do the best he can with his God-given abilities, that he can feel secure and comfortable, able to interact with others, to grow and change. This self-acceptance, or self-love is part of the great commandments with which we are well acquainted, which infer that only the self-accepting individual can accept others; one must love oneself to be able to love one's neighbor. Dr. Glasser, prominent educator, says much the same thing in psychological terms: "When man acts in such a way that he gives and receives love and feels worthwhile to himself and others, his behavior is right and moral." Rollo May points out in *Love and Will* the importance and meaning of self-love when he states that it is the opposite of selfishness and self-centeredness: "Love of self means having sense of one's own worth as a person and as a child of God. It is from this base that we can reach out generously to others."

As I look back over these first pages, I note that references to individuals from two entirely different groups seem strangely interwoven. Both the theologian or religious thinker and the psychologist seem to be expressing the same concerns over the search for the good, contributive life and the self-realization of each human individual.

Canon J. B. Phillips, a well-known clergyman in the Church of England, recently expressed great satisfaction in the acceptance of the Christian Faith by many psychologists as one of the essentials of a healthy life. It is my belief that authorities in the Church and psychiatric settings would agree that if a human being is to feel secure and fulfilled, he needs to love and be loved. Most are also convinced of the significance of a deeper need experienced by man in his solitary state: To love and be loved by God, to be firmly convinced that he is a son of God and that nothing can break this relationship.

This almost parallel thinking in terms of the *religiously* sound life and the *psychologically* sound life, so intrigued me that I found myself selecting four salient aspects of the human person and then searching for similar statements from both sides. I disclose my findings here because I am convinced that they will give the same breadth and perspective to other youth-oriented work goals as they have to mine.

1. THE NEED FOR HUMAN RELATIONSHIPS AND UNDERSTANDING

Psychologist

We need to speak through the language of relationships as well as through the language of words . . . my friendliness helps you to become friendly. My anxiety causes you to be anxious.

Reuel L. Howe (Psychologist and Priest)

Theologian

Even the least intelligent of men are beginning to see that unless they love and understand one another, they will most certainly destroy one another. . . . What ultimately matters is . . . the way in which we behave toward other people. . . .

J. B. Phillips (Priest)

2. THE NEED FOR COMPASSION

Compassion is an essential feature of mental health, emotional maturity, and acceptance of self and others . . . to be compassionate represents a high level of maturity. . . .

A. T. Jersild (Psychologist)

The most hopeful place in which to build a bridge between the worlds of faith and unfaith is on the common ground of human compassion. . . .

J. B. Phillips (Priest)

3. THE NEED FOR LOVING, CARING, FEELING

Many people avoid personal subjects for fear of the emotions they may arouse . . . for fear of having their hearts touched. . . . A false feeling of shame about the emotions is very widespread . . . often even joy is smothered. . . .

Paul Tournier (Psychiatrist)

[We] need someone in and through whom we can find "atoneness" . . . our need is for love, acceptance and discipline. . . . Love, in the highest sense comes from God . . . only as we have His gift of love, can we have the power and ability to meet the terrible demand to love and the demand for love. . . .

Reuel Howe (Priest)

4. THE NEED FOR ACCEPTANCE OF SELF AND OTHERS

Self-acceptance and understanding of self are closely associated . . . to accept himself, the growing person must be aware of himself. . . . The way he feels about himself will depend on the way others feel about him. . . .

A. T. Jersild (Psychologist)

We cannot love others unless we have a healthy love of ourselves . . .

Erich Fromm (Psychologist)

A Christian is one who can both praise God for salvation and confess that he is a sinner without being dismayed. . . . We can accept ourselves because God accepts us . . . and we can accept and love one another, too. . . .

Reuel Howe (Priest)

It is indeed encouraging to the layman to discover that, in this materialistic, technological age of ours, there are so many points on which the scientist, the psychologist and the medical man agree with the philosopher and theologian, as they search for ways to improve the state of mankind.

2

Drama:
One Solution

The history of the theater begins long before Christ. Greek dramas were both theater and worship experiences; they sent their audiences away purged of base emotions, which Aristotle describes as *catharsis*. In the Early Church the power of drama to touch men deeply and turn them to God was recognized and used. It has always been considered the art through which men express themselves in action. Many of the biblical prophets used dramatization to bring vital truths before the people. Moses reminded the Israelites of the passing of the death angel by instituting the ceremonial killing of the Passover lamb. He also initiated the Feast of the Tabernacles, which the Jews observed by the symbolic breaking of palm and willow branches. The whole liturgy of the early Church is dramatic in nature. Jesus' life and death, his institution of the practice of the Lord's supper all combine in a divine drama of redemption.

Other records exist, testifying to the close kinship of drama and the early church. In the fourth century, Appolinarius, priest of Laodicea, recast large segments of the Old Testament into dramatic form and later his son did the same with the New Testament. One of the first known ecclesiastical dramatists was Romanus of Byzantium. Later, Ignatius, Deacon of St. Sophia's, wrote a dramatized version of *Man's First Transgression*. It was not until the Middle Ages, however, when the Church began to emphasize the dramatic element lying at the core of its ritual, that modern drama was born. The Passion Play of the thirteenth and fourteenth centuries evolved from the religious service itself and became the most potent force in medieval civilization. The statement has been made that definite dramatic expression follows the inherent impulse to worship. That cannot be questioned, whether one refers for proof to the origin of Greek drama or that of the Christian world. Mystery plays were presented based on stories from the Bible; Miracle plays, many of which were accompanied by the finest sacred music, were drawn from the lives of the saints and were presented in the chancel itself. Then, at the end of the fifteenth century, as secular material became more popular, theatrical performances were moved out of the church and played on the porticoes or on street corners by the medieval craft guilds.

From this time on, drama fell into disrepute with church authorities. In Dr. Harry Emerson Fosdick's words: ". . . drama, which began as a child of the church, grew up to be its prodigal son." Some believe, even today, that theater will never again find itself until it finds its soul in a religious source. Recently, one could take heart in watching definite steps being taken toward a new alliance between church and theater. The recognition of the need for discovering a force which can capture the minds and imaginations of men and lead them back to the belief that spiritual idealism should be the motivating power of life is universal. And why not the drama experience? As Elizabeth Edland says: "Outside of personal experience, drama is the most powerful teaching medium . . . just what use the church makes of this depends wholly on itself. What a fine, healthy cooperation between these two forces can accomplish has yet to be seen."

Martha Candler, in her book *Drama In Religious Service*, tells an amazing and touching story of a little New England town, Pomfret, Connecticut, which has produced a true drama of worship each Christmas since 1912. One can see the deep spiritual inspiration it brings to the whole countryside when one reads what a pious old lady, watching the movement of a gifted young dancer portraying the Angel of the Lord, said: "Such beauty . . . certainly draws one closer to God." Another participant writes of the same celebration: "There is something in human nature which is touched by the simple miracle and responds with the simplicity of the heart of a child . . . the play is as much a service, and as little a show, as on the day it was inaugurated."

Dr. Harold Ehrensperger firmly believes that drama must play an important part in religious education. He feels that there is little point in accumulating fine sentiments in church school and youth fellowships unless we so cultivate the dramatic instinct that we can identify ourselves with life situations in which these worthy philosophies and values come alive. It is a learning-through-doing technique which he recommends and most educators support. Drama is a medium which can make eternal truths become vivid and real.

Before taking a close look at its use as an aid in vitalizing Christian education, I feel impelled to address you, my readers, concerning our mutual goals. I believe that I can assume that we, as Christian teachers, set some basic objectives for ourselves that are unique. I am even bold enough to attempt to state them in a single sentence. WE STRIVE TO MAKE GOD THE CENTER OF OUR LIVES, AND TO

FIND WAYS TO BRING HIS REALITY INTO THE LIVES OF OTHERS. This way of life, has been described as "man's reach for the highest and noblest existence possible." Most of us search diligently for means which will help us discover the redeeming power of God's love and witness it in action in our lives. Motivated by this philosophy, we can hope to achieve our educational goals: to enrich the child's concepts of life so that through growth in body, mind, and spirit, he may become a happy, contributive adult.

Scientific research in the field of human development has offered significant guideposts which point out the need to focus attention on the growth of the integrated personality. Further studies testify to the fact that a person can only become whole when he is motivated by an ideal. For the Christian, this ideal lies in a life that finds its source of power in God and through the teachings and example of Jesus' life, finds a right relationship to man. The child must be helped to attain the fullest self-realization, through opportunities to use his inner urges to create and imagine, as well as experience social situations which will bring about a deepening of sympathetic understanding and a secure sense of belonging. Thus will these two basic human needs, essential to the healthy, happy life be realized: 1) the need for self-fulfillment (love of self); 2) the need for acceptance of one's fellow man (love of neighbor).

CREATIVE DRAMA — AN EFFECTIVE TOOL

As one considers incorporating drama in the church program, three categories automatically come to mind:

(a) Creative drama, or the spontaneous communication of thought and feeling. This informal drama is most appropriate for use in the church school class, the youth fellowship, the scout group and similar organizations.

(b) The play, presented before an audience, written and produced to provide a rewarding spiritual experience. Such a presentation need not be based on biblical material but should, as one author has said: ". . . send an audience away exalted in mood, and with a deepened sense of God and man."

(c) The dramatic worship service which can move its participants and deepen the meaning of the gospel message.

Because creative drama has proven to be the most effective tool in achieving the educational objectives already discussed, and in motivating well-rounded growth and development, this subject is treated in detail. Later chapters will give suggestions and guidelines for presenting the formal play. Several small plays, which have been developed creatively and produced, are included for those who prefer to work from a manuscript.

Common sense urges the wise teacher to make use of the dramatic instinct which exists in every human being and has been a fundamental developmental force since the world began. This instinct, which constantly spurs the imagination to work, helps an individual to put himself in someone else's shoes. The more others' life situations are experienced imaginatively, the deeper one's perspective and human understanding becomes.

If we are to be sensitive to other men, we must have the power to imagine. Regarding the significance of an active imagination, it has been said that the need of learning how best to direct the power of the imagination is the greatest need which the world faces today. Many feel that an education which deals primarily with the soul, the spirit and the imagination is the only education which is worthwhile. Dame Sybil Thorndike, renowned British actress, described the imaginative actor this way: " . . . acting is an art which can help build human beings [into] . . . sensitive creatures, able to feel the joys and sorrows of others as their own . . . by living in the lives of others, with an eye and a mind imaginatively tuned and objective, they may effect real cures for their own failures."

Because it is essential that the term CREATIVE DRAMATICS, as it will be used in this volume, be clearly understood, a simple, all-inclusive definition is stated here: CREATIVE DRAMATICS IS THE EXPRESSION OF THOUGHT AND FEELING IN ONE'S OWN TERMS, THROUGH ACTION, SPEECH, OR BOTH. Obviously, the above description is the direct counterpart of formal drama, the performance of the written play. In such a presentation, the thoughts and feelings expressed are those of an adult playwright, memorized from a printed text. The manner in which they are expressed by the actor is determined by the teacher-director rather than the player himself; usually voice inflections and movements on stage are dictated rather than spontaneous. A young person who must read lines and move about according to specific directions can give little of his own interpretation to a character. His work is more like the response of a perfectly controlled puppet. A greater challenge to the imagination and wider opportunity for personal growth are provided by the creative drama experience where such limitations do not exist.

In the spontaneous, improvised scene, the child has an opportunity to develop his own ideas in speech and action. Because his expression is based upon his own thoughts and feelings, it is fresh, natural, and believable.

Experience has proven that the following attributes, so essential to religious living, can be reinforced through this activity: a) acceptance of and love for one's self; b) a deep understanding of one's fellow man; c) an active, creative imagination; d) released, and therefore balanced, emotions; e) independent thinking, resourcefulness, initiative; f) sensitivity to beauty of sound, color and line; g) coordination and effectiveness of body and voice communication. If a few or all of these characteristics can result from a continuing creative drama experience, the practice surely deserves a place among our favorite educational tools. Its unusual powers are recognized by many authorities, one of whom has said, " . . . an individual learns to the extent that he lives an experience." It has been scientifically proven that one makes an idea his own when he feels it in his heart and lets it motivate him to action. A child who has played through a scene in which he is helping out at home in an emergency, giving up a prized possession for someone less fortunate, or turning aside from his own game to aid someone in distress, experiences a sense of well-being, an inner joy and satisfaction. This is the sign of spiritual growth. Moments such as these come alive in creative dramatization. The same situations, read about or heard, cannot evoke as deep or lasting a response. As children have repeated opportunities to feel the joys, hopes, sorrows and fears of other human beings, they gain insight and understanding which is stored in the subconscious and spontaneously recalled, later, to help them cope effectively with similar problems. Trying on other characters, imagining their reactions to varied situations, gives one a deep, sympathetic understanding of how other people live, feel and relate. The plight of the refugee, the orphan, the lonely, poor little rich girl, take on new meaning through dramatization. Exploring various solutions for human problems develops sensitivity, awareness and independent thinking. A dedicated colleague said this very well in the "creed" she suggested many years ago for our experiments in the use of drama in education at Johns Hopkins University: PLAYACTING IS THE CHILD'S REHEARSAL FOR HIS ROLE AS A GROWN-UP.

Finally, let us note that during this kind of activity all three facets of the human person — mind, body and spirit (emotions) are being simultaneously called into play. Since research in child development testifies to the interdependence of the three — the health of one being closely related to that of the other — it would appear desirable to promote this three-fold growth through the creative drama experience. At once, the mind thinks, the heart feels and these thoughts and emotions are expressed in bodily action.

3

The Successful Teacher
A Self-Analysis

At the outset, let us state a well-worn truth which bears repeating again and again: THE SUCCESS OF ANY PROJECT IS LARGELY DEPENDENT UPON THE QUALITY OF THE LEADERSHIP. The teacher must, then, consider carefully not only the benefits of the creative drama experience and the characteristics and attitudes he or she is trying to foster, but also his or her own personal qualifications. Helping little ones to enrich their lives, to become "small saints," is a serious responsibility as well as a great privilege. Some beautiful words, left anonymously on my desk one morning during a workshop for the Association of Childhood Education, express this awe which many people justifiably feel as they gently but firmly set out to guide young lives.

"I saw tomorrow passing by on little children's feet,
And in their forms and faces read her prophecy complete.
I saw tomorrow look at me from little children's eyes,
And thought, 'How carefully we'd teach if we were wise.' "

We must be wise in so many ways. Above all, every good teacher must strive to achieve emotional maturity and to have no concern with self-pride or self-aggrandizement. He must be a friend of those he teaches, loving warmly and constantly. As Socrates said, "One can only teach whom one loves." Many years of experience have proven the truth of a related corollary: "One can only learn from one whom one loves." The ideal leader will listen earnestly, striving to organize the thinking of others quickly, always working to create an atmosphere free from tension and gentle with friendship and understanding, where everyone will soon feel secure and accepted for what he is. As Dr. McCaslin says: "In his acceptance of every child and what he has to offer, the leader has taken the first big step toward building self-confidence." The conscientious teacher will always bend every effort to help each child to develop a good concept of himself; in this healthy self-image lies his success in exploring his world. Only when a child accepts or "loves" himself can he feel secure enough to experiment, discover, adventure, reach out and share with his neighbors.

The teacher who can successfully create this warm climate, where children feel free to work and play together, will need certain personal attributes. He must be completely objective, unbiased, enthusiastic, patient and imaginative. Above all, he must love and believe in children, eagerly strive to spark their latent creative powers and bring each one to the threshold of his own special capacity. Successful creative drama teachers have a basic philosophy in common. Geraldine Siks, a gifted drama teacher, describes very aptly this certain "something" which they all seem to share. She says: "they have a friendly attitude toward humanity and a creative attitude of enjoyment for their work . . . a genuine love for children and a deep belief and enjoyment in drama." Dr. Ehrensperger, an authority in the field, has outlined clearly the attributes of a successful religious drama director: "1) He must be an expert in the proper study of mankind, which is MAN; 2) he should be capable of an all-round understanding of people; 3) he should have sensitivity for the feelings of people; 4) he should have sufficient objectivity about his work; 5) he must put first the growth of his co-workers and second the artistry of his project; 6) he will understand that the result . . . achieved in individual growth and religious experience . . . is the most satisfying compensation; 7) he must believe in the religious value of the dramatic process; 8) whatever else may be prerequisite . . . a 'sense of humor is a saving grace; 9) he should have a 'sense of theater' . . . there is no substitute for knowledge and competence in this field."

A very special quality to which few teachers give serious consideration — possibly because it is intangible — is what we have referred to in these pages as GOODNESS. Geraldine Siks calls it GREATNESS. She believes that " . . . greatness lies in the kind of person one is and strives to become, what he says and does . . . and feels and believes in. His way of living is reflected in his appearance, language, attitudes . . . his sense of values, integrity and humor." How true it is that the teacher who brings this kind of greatness of spirit into his classroom will soon find his students reflecting the same qualities and attitudes. He will have created a climate in which creativity can flourish — a friendly, vital, exciting place, permeated with love and compassion. A love for and understanding of the art of drama is essential for the successful teacher. Only when he has experienced the beauty and power of the theater, can he hope to motivate young people to communicate creatively. Some training in creative drama techniques, observation of skilled leaders at work and comprehensive reading on the subject are also recommended. Robert Edmond Jones, in *The Dramatic Imagination* expresses eloquently the basic love for the theater so essential for the good teacher. He says that " . . . of all attitudes one can have toward life, the 'theatrical' attitude is the most truly creative . . . we are still lost in wonder before this magical art of the theater. We call it glamour, or poetry, or romance, but that doesn't explain it. In some mysterious way, these old, simple, ancestral needs still survive in us, and an actor can make them live again for a while. We become children once more . . . we believe."

4

Creative Drama
The First Steps

Whether the religious educator plans to use creative drama 1) to vitalize the lesson in the Church school, or 2) as one of the activities of the youth fellowship, or 3) in a separate program designed to motivate human development and further Christian living, certain fundamental principles — basic to all situations — should be carefully considered:

First — Personal growth, like that of the delicate plant, does not occur overnight. Education is a continuing, dynamic process, freeing emotional tension, relaxing tight muscles, building inner security and stirring creative imagination into activity. All require time, patience and a carefully planned program.

Second — A group or class of approximately the same age level, and of manageable size, (15-20 is ideal), should meet with the same teacher, in the same place, once a week if possible, for the entire school year. The facility, or classroom, should be bright, informal and provide ample space for free movement.

Third — The gradual flowering of the human personality depends upon an even and sustaining climate of warm friendliness and a regular week-by-week nourishment of the roots of the young "plant."

Fourth — For best results, a definite progressive plan, a step-by-step procedure, based on the laws of natural physical growth, should be followed. Each step, from simple pantomime to improvised dialogue, makes greater demands upon the creative stones, which, when used in the suggested order, build a firm, sure path leading to the growth of the whole personality. Every teacher will determine his own method of shaping and polishing each stone, seeking material appropriate to his participants' capacities and interests.

In this chapter, the first three steps of creative drama are introduced. These exercises in simple pantomime are essential in the progression from creative play to drama.

THE FIRST STEP — BUILDING THE ATMOSPHERE

To enjoy a meal to the fullest extent, one requires spotless linen, good food and pleasant surroundings. The success of the creative drama class, too, depends upon attendant circumstances. In a cheerful, quiet place where the informal atmosphere breaks down tensions and encourages active participation, exciting things can happen. Only in this kind of climate, where one feels a sense of belonging, can the creative impulse be released. In this atmosphere of mutual respect, each individual can express his concerns without fear of ridicule or unjust criticism. Ideas flow, feelings are communicated, opinions are shared, and through sharing, exchanged. The responsibility for creating this atmosphere rests, largely, with the leader of the group. It is the enthusiastic co-worker, not the cold disciplinarian, the patient, cheerful friend, not the impatient, bored teacher, who will inspire the confidence on which the creative drama project thrives. In this kind of climate, there will be few discipline problems. Unfortunately, there is no one recipe for developing such a climate. In fact, there are as many different approaches as there are leaders. Each individual brings different personal qualities and talents to the task. An explanation of my own method, used in our original child drama projects and started as an educational experiment on the campus of Johns Hopkins University in Baltimore, might prove helpful.

Let us imagine a group of eight-to-ten-year-olds gathered on a Saturday morning for a creative drama session. Many of them have never seen one another before. (The same might be true of an opening church school class). The teacher begins: "How nice that we all found our way here; and what a great morning it is, too." A few general comments follow, about where we come from, how far we had to go, who brought us, and the like. As soon as everyone has joined in the conversation and seems comfortably settled on rugs, couches and low chairs that have previously been arranged informally, the leader's remarks take a different path: "It's fine to have such a big children's theater family this year. Do you know how many we are?" They look about trying to count as the leader continues: "We are not all here, you know. There are seven other groups just like yours. Altogether we're about a hundred and fifty strong. Think of that! Some are big children, some are little and some are middle-sized." There are "ohs" and "ahs" at this revelation. "Yes, indeed, I have so many children that I feel a bit like the Old Woman Who Lived in The Shoe. But there's one big difference: I *do* know what to do with all my children; I love every one of them and I'm so thankful for each boy and girl in our family."

Then this talk of the "family," and what makes a good member of a family begins. "What is a good scout in your troop like?" "Why do you enjoy certain members of your class so much?" Through carefully phrased questions and guided discussion, spontaneous responses like these are evoked. "I like people who aren't always interested in themselves," or "the people who share their toys are fun!" You may hear: "The best friends I have in school are those who care about me and what I'm interested in" or "in our family the ones who are best liked are those who help, not the ones who always make excuses for not doing any work." Before long, certain basic principles and conclusions will have surfaced:

(1) To be a good member of a family, our family or any group, I must forget "self" and try to think of and enjoy others in the group.

(2) I will try to be aware of ways in which I can help others to be happy; I will find a lot of joy in sharing responsibilities.

(3) Since this is our home where we meet once a week, I will try to think of ways to take care of it, then I will enjoy it more.

A short step leads the discussion to the next significant point: "How is forgetting one's self related to play-acting or make-believe?" Frequently, someone will make the perfect reply, "Well, if you're pretending to be somebody else, you have to forget yourself, then you really can be somebody else for a while." Even if this or a similar answer is not immediately forthcoming, a few more carefully worded questions will bring the conversation to this conclusion. It will be obvious that the friendly family atmosphere has been established; everyone feels that he belongs. Even if he doesn't quite fit the pattern of a good family member, he has a recipe for becoming one. Now, at long last, the group is ready to work on the second step — the pantomiming of simple activities.

The above example may give the impression that the warm, friendly climate has been easily developed, as if by magic, in the first few minutes of the first meeting. This is not always the case. Each leader faces different problems, different and perhaps hard-to-reach personalities, and differing time periods allotted to creative dramatics. He will accept the challenge, remembering only that no progress can be made until the climate is right.

THE SECOND STEP — SIMPLE PANTOMIME

The word *pantomime* means the expression of an idea through action alone, unassisted by the spoken word. This kind of play-acting may be performed on many levels. From the simple action of bouncing an imaginary ball or picking a flower to a complex scene involving several people which tells a complete story. It is wise to begin with the pantomiming of familiar, simple activities, easily accessible in the storehouse of the imagination. This is really only dramatic play, having none of the form limitations which one associates with drama; in picking flowers, building sand castles or snow forts, there is no conflict, no beginning, climax or denouement. It is simply a kind of make-believe, an expression of the play instinct, with which the Creator has richly endowed each child at birth. The emphasis, during this part of the study, is three-fold: 1) activating the imagination, 2) developing concentration, 3) freeing the body by encouraging natural, spontaneous response to imaginary stimuli. As an individual imaginatively recreates a place, an object, or experience, new thoughts will set his body in motion. His physical movement, thus motivated, will be free and coordinated because it is self-directed rather than adult-imposed. A simple exercise like gathering a bunch of daisies, filling a bucket at an old well, or building sand castles might seem too simple to the un-initiated teacher. He will soon discover, however, that although this appears to be elementary in nature, the art of pretending believably is sufficiently difficult to master that it warrants the expenditure of considerable time.

In selecting material, it is advisable to use situations where there is a suggestion of service, sharing or participating in family or group activities. Natural opportunities are thus provided for a discussion of the joy that comes in working together, the fun derived from sharing the common task. One must constantly keep in mind socio-economic background and the interest levels of the group if the material content is to challenge and inspire. Children living close to the ocean might enjoy playing in the sand or collecting shells; another mountain-bred group, having never seen a beach, might feel bored or insecure working with such material. They should not be asked to recreate, in their imaginations, a place which they have never seen.

Many years ago, when I was beginning to experiment with creative dramatics, a group of inner city children taught me the fallacy of using unfamiliar material. I learned the hard way; but the painful lesson was driven home; and I have never made the same mistake again. The story may be worth repeating here. It was autumn, and, as I drove into the city, I was deeply impressed by the bright color of falling leaves. At once, I decided to use this visual impression in an opening exercise. I spoke to the children of the lovely colors and the great fun it was to jump into a huge pile of leaves in the fall. I was so interested in my subject, that I didn't notice the blank expressions on those small faces. So I continued: "Each of you take one of those rakes, now . . . see . . . there are a lot of them leaning against the wall (I indicated the direction). And then everybody will rake up a big pile of these crispy leaves that are all over the ground." There was an uncomfortable silence. Nobody moved! I urged them: "Run along, get your rakes . . . " They tried, poor things. They moved, in unison, to the wall which I had pointed out. There they stopped, looking helplessly at one another. Finally, one bold ten and a half year old spoke: " 'Scuse me, Miss, but we don't know what a rake is . . . never see'd a pile of leaves . . . We don't know how to pick up a rake 'cause, well, how can we when we never see'd one?" I was covered with embarrassment and chagrin. I had committed an unpardonable sin. I had expected these underprivileged children to recreate a scene which was a complete mystery to them. I did apologize, and we immediately replaced the assignment with something more appropriate, something within the range of their own experience. I trust my lesson can serve to make the point.

Another helpful hint for the beginning class concerns the use of the two "keys" to the "secret treasure chest" of pretending. We use the term "secret keys" because children so enjoy secret codes, the discovery of buried treasure, hiding plans for club meetings and the like. The first "key" is *make a mind picture,* and the second, *think the thoughts of the character you're pretending to be.* Providing these "helps" or "clues" at the earliest meeting of the group will often persuade even the most inhibited student to begin to play. The first key implies the need for clearly replacing all people and things present with imaginary people and things in the scene to be played. For example, in order to gather shells at the beach, we must see in our minds the blue sky, the lovely blue-green ocean, and the white foam of the breaking waves curling up onto the sand. All other people and things about us must go! No longer is there a classroom, a rug on the floor, chairs, desks, tables. The second key urges one to silence his own mental processes so that the thought patterns of the assumed

character may take full possession. It is soon obvious, perhaps with some demonstrations by the leader, that thoughts motivate body action. When one thinks, "Oh, look over there! That's a beautiful shell," one automatically runs across the sand and bends down to examine the treasure. These two keys are the core of believable, sincere pantomime. It is wise to recall them again and again as the work proceeds. A simple question like, "What were you thinking when you saw the little bird fall from the nest?" will stimulate the thought processes and lead to genuine, convincing action.

All of the early exercises should be done with groups; each child working as an individual, but playing within the comforting framework of the group. If the classroom is large, some exercises can use the entire class. For example, in a large recreation room, all eighteen children in a class might carry a bucket and look for shells at the beach at the same time. If the space is limited, the use of three groups of six will solve the problem. After the first group has finished and brought the buckets of shells back to some designated place, an open discussion or critique will be useful. The leader should always begin the conversation with an affirmative statement: "That was *lovely*. You were enjoying that warm sunshine so much, I wish I could have been there, too." All the observers, and perhaps even the participants themselves, will soon get into the evaluation. Some questions and statements like this are likely to be forthcoming during an evaluation of the first group's playing of the beach scene:

"Do we have to put our shells into the bucket?"
"Couldn't we put them in our pockets?"
"Some people found so many shells, some only two or three. Can't we decide on how many?"
"I saw somebody go very close to the water. I hope he was barefoot."

The leader considers each question and answers it thoughtfully. He will have learned something very significant from some of them. Obviously, in describing the beach and the water line, where the buckets were, how many shells were to be gathered, he had not been quite clear. In the beginning, children will feel much more secure if every detail of a scene is explained and the placement of each unit made very clear. When they are working in a group, the members must know exactly where everything is located, for we are asking them to see the beach, and for the sake of the observers, too, they must all be making the same MIND PICTURE.

The evaluation over, the second group is ready to try the same pantomime. Another critique follows. So the class proceeds until each child has had his turn. This evaluation plan can be mutually beneficial to players and observers alike, if it is skillfully guided. The audience members of the class learn to give concentrated attention to the work of their colleagues, as soon as it becomes evident that their comments and constructive criticisms are welcomed and respected. The young players, on the other hand, gain in stature through the valuable experience of learning to take these suggestions in good spirit.

One gentle reminder to the leader may be in order. In any group, one or two children, usually those who are less secure, will offer only negative criticism of their peers. This must never be tolerated. The sensitive leader will find a way to handle this delicate situation wisely. "Perhaps you didn't watch carefully enough, Jane," he might say. "I think I saw each of Bobby's shells go into his bucket. We must remember, if we are to be good members of our family, to make only the kinds of suggestions that are helpful. Better watch closely the next time."

A high level of interest will be maintained throughout the entire class provided the leader has prepared his lesson plan carefully and has many ideas for activity pantomime ready for the forty-five-minute to one-hour class period. The next few meetings will proceed in somewhat the same manner. Although the sessions still concern the pantomiming of simple activities, the approach to the assignments may vary. Several techniques which have proved successful follow:

(1) He may divide his class of eighteen into two groups by counting off by nine. The number ones in each group will raise their hands and take a good long look at each other so that they will remember their partners. Each of the other pairs of two will do the same. The first group of nine will go to an imaginary store counter which has been carefully designated by the leader, and described to the children in detail. Toys and things to wear are sold here but with no cost to the customer; he need only select what he wants and take it along. As he turns away from the counter, he must handle his purchase carefully so that his partner can see it quite clearly. The partner will take the object and will indicate, by his pantomime, whether he has discovered what it is. This exercise, which resembles a guessing game, demands clear visualization and concentration. When the first group has finished with its trip to the store and the work has been discussed, the second group of nine repeats the performance.

(2) This time the children may all be seated in a large circle. The leader says, "Now I have a beautiful big tray here (he pantomimes picking up a long tray), and it's full of delicious things to eat and drink. I will pass it around to each of you, for I am delighted you came to see me. I want you to take just one thing, please, to be sure I have enough. Don't start to eat or drink until everyone has been served. That's much more polite! Then, when I put the tray down, I want you to enjoy

"It's a lovely box of fudge!" A group of fifth-grade children get a creative drama lesson from the author at a recent teachers' workshop.

your refreshments and I'm going to try to guess what you have selected." This again requires "making a mind picture" as well as deciding on which article to select. It is still simple pantomime; it does, however, make some demands upon the leader!

It may be wise to mention certain difficulties which occur from time to time during even the most carefully planned pantomime lessons. Some of the more reserved children who have been conditioned to obey rigid rules of behavior may be hesitant in participating at first. If they actually refuse to join any group, some casual remark from the leader may prove helpful. He might say, "You think you're not quite ready to work on this little scene, Susan? That's quite all right. We'd like to have your opinion about it when we've finished; your comments will be helpful, I know." This kind of attitude will remove any guilt feelings Susan may have and may also give her a feeling of belonging because her comments are wanted. She is playing an important part, even though she is not working with the rest. Other children who lack confidence may offer to join the group only after watching their neighbors' work and copying it, if possible, hoping to win approval and avoid criticism. They can be helped gradually to overcome these fears if the leader assures everyone that there is no right and wrong way to gather shells or pick flowers. Everyone sees different shells and different flowers. Certainly each will take a different length of time to gather them and each will handle them in a different manner. What is most important is that everyone makes a picture in his mind and believes in what he is doing.

Another problem may present itself when a giggle or a loud whisper comes from those observing. If this occurs, the exercise should be stopped immediately with a firm but quiet suggestion from the leader: "I'm sorry, but I am afraid that we will have to stop and start our exercise again. You know when there is any noise at all — a cough, a laugh, or even a whisper — our mind pictures go away. We're back here in the classroom instead of in the garden (or beach, or cave, or wherever the scene is set). So we'll start again from the beginning. Do please remember, friends, that we who are watching must be still as mice. When our turn comes, we don't want others who are watching us to wipe out our mind pictures, do we? Then let's be as thoughtful of this group working now as we want them to be when we try the scene later." This is an excellent opportunity to drive home the principles of the Golden Rule. They will soon learn to extend this courtesy to one another.

Occasionally, when two or three in a group of six finish their exercise very quickly, they have a tendency to hurry off to their seats. This movement through the acting area may completely disturb the concentration of those still working. It is therefore advisable to suggest at the outset something like the following: "If anyone finishes picking apples (or gathering flowers, shells or whatever) while the rest are working, please just stay where you are, sitting or standing quietly until everyone has completed the scene." If a scene such as gathering a bucketful of stones seems to have no ending, the leader should tell the children ahead of time that he will use some single exclamation such as "curtain!" to end the activity.

It is difficult to state arbitrarily the exact number of sessions which should be devoted to simple pantomime, the second step. The frequency, as well as the length of the meetings, will influence one's decision. The readiness of the group determines the time to proceed to the next step, MOOD PANTOMIME. When most of the children are participating freely in both the exercises and the discussions, and they are concentrating enough to picture in their minds and let the thoughts of another character motivate believable and coordinated movement, the time has come to move on to more complex work.

The following list of simple pantomime materials for several age groups may serve as models for the church school teacher. They are not adequate for use during all of the sessions which one may devote to simple pantomime; they are only intended to guide and assist. Ideas are given in abbreviated form to save space. The leader must find his own way to introduce the material to his children in an interesting and appropriate manner. For example, in using the first exercise, one would not say, "Gather twigs for the fire." A more inspiring approach might go like this: "You have gone out with your family and neighbors for a picnic down by the river and after you've had your sandwiches and cake, when the sun has gone down, it has become quite chilly. Your mother says, 'Well, I had better go to the edge of the woods and gather some bits of wood so we can start a little fire.' Knowing that Mother has already done all the work to prepare your picnic, you stop playing ball and offer at once to help by gathering the sticks. Now, here is the spot where you are going to build the fire (indicating the spot), and, over there, along the wall, by the door, is the edge of the forest where you will find lots of dried sticks. So will everyone go to collect six or seven sticks and bring them back here to the wood pile? Whenever you are ready, with the picture in your mind, begin." This kind of introduction helps to give meaning to their single activity.

For Ages Eight To Ten

1. Gathering twigs for a fire.
2. Bouncing a new ball.
3. Skipping rope.
4. Feeding the fish (birds, etc.).
5. Building a sand castle.
6. Working on a jigsaw puzzle.
7. Picking flowers for Mother's birthday.
8. Planting seeds in the garden.

For Ages Eleven To Thirteen

1. Threading a needle.
2. Sealing, addressing, and stamping a letter.
3. Arranging flowers in a vase.
4. Setting the table for Mother's guests.

5. Packing bathing suit and towel for a swimming trip.
6. Helping to clean the bookcase by dusting and replacing the books on the shelf.
7. Making a jelly sandwich for little sister's lunch.
8. Filling a bucket with soil to help Mother fix her flower bed.

THE THIRD STEP: MOOD PANTOMIME

During the work in simple pantomime, no mention has been made of communicating feelings. The fact that one's bodily movements change as one's moods change has not yet been approached. Now, when everyone has developed some facility in picturing himself in many different locations, it is time to begin this more complicated matter of expressing feelings. It is best to take some exercise already attempted like collecting shells or gathering firewood and discuss how the movement pattern would change as one's feelings change. It is easy to see how different a child's movements would be if, for instance, when gathering twigs for a fire, he was lost with two friends on a mountain trail. His actions are swift, tense and jerky. His anxiety as to how they will get through the cold night governs his body and facial reactions. More importantly, his thought patterns, those of the frightened, lost boy, control every muscle of his body. The leader must point out the fact that only when the mind picture is clear and the thought patterns real will the body movements be convincing enough to tell the story.

In this technological age, one must explore rather than neglect opportunities to help children toward a fuller realization of their emotional life. Wesner Fallaw in *The Modern Parent and the Teaching Church*, expresses deep concern over a world which is attuned to the secular rather than a sacred wave-length. He blames this unhappy state on undue adulation for intellectual communication and neglect or scorn of emotional expression. This fact, though stated by educators and psychologists for a long time, is largely disregarded today. From infancy, the child naturally expresses emotion, at first in an aimless, random way, later in a more clearly defined fashion. But many children are urged by adults around them to restrain their show of emotions. They are pressured to calm down or to stop crying, and are warned that it isn't acceptable to get angry or to be afraid. Such insistence that a child conceal his feelings is often damaging to his natural growth. Frequently, they are quite different from those he presents publicly. So suspect is the show of feelings today that one can but wonder whether our early American puritanical heritage is partially to blame. This dilemma is presented clearly by Arthur Jersild in his book, *Child Psychology*. He deplores an educational system which eagerly promotes all kinds of learning except knowledge of our own and others' feelings. For most of us, who have been deprived of such knowledge, it is difficult to understand or foster healthy, emotional growth in our children.

It is indeed a dilemma, for the healthy, sensitive, responsive individual *must* be able to express his deepest feelings if he is to relate comfortably to his fellow man. The emotions need to be kept supple and active. If they are not exercised, we become numb, wooden creatures without the capacity for sensitivity and compassion. The thought of deliberately providing opportunities to show fear, anger, hate and the other negative emotions disturbs some people. One must hasten to make a very strong case in favor of using such material for creative drama. Since we all have these feelings from time to time, it seems wiser and safer to "let off steam" by expressing them in the controllable, non-threatening improvisational setting. A certain healthy catharsis is the inevitable result. In their book, *Teaching Drama*, two British educational drama specialists, R. N. Pemberton-Billing and J. D. Clegg, underline this theory with a graphic example: "The throwing of a stone through an unpleasant neighbor's window is much better done in pretense in drama than with a real stone in actuality. There is ample evidence to show that enacting the deed in pretense reduces the impulse to do it in reality. The playing out of these emotions should lead to a realization of their inadequacy and stimulate the desire to replace them with something better." The religious educator should assume the serious responsibility of encouraging this facet of human development.

SHARPENING SENSITIVITY

Every thought and feeling that gives meaning to life enters the mind and heart through one or more of the senses or some remembered sense impression. A sensitive individual is at once aware, concerned and responsive. His senses reach out and absorb impressions to which he responds by expressing his thoughts and feelings. One of the unfortunate effects of the technological, push-button efficiency of modern life is a dulling of the senses. An individual is often unwittingly in danger of becoming a robot, with eyes that see not and ears that hear not. If children are to retain their sensitivity, they must be provided with experiences which keep the five senses alive and active. Since this *mood pantomime* stage in the creative drama project deals with the emotions, it seems appropriate at this point to introduce *sense exercises.* One of the best ways to approach the subject is to encourage the careful observation of and concentration on sights, sounds, smells, tastes and how things feel. From a deep absorption and involvement with *things,* one progresses naturally to a deeper relationship with *people.* A few suggestions for beginning sense exercises may be helpful.

Looking

(a) Use words to motivate picturing. Ask questions such as: "What do you see in your mind when I say: 'MOTHER, FRIEND, THANKSGIVING, WINTER, FIRE'?"

(b) Recall experiences: "Tell me something special you noticed on your way to church school. What colors did you see that were exciting?"

(c) Sharper ability to observe: "Look around you for a moment. How many curved lines do you see? Where is the color blue or green used (or red or yellow)?"

(d) Try more detailed and concentrated observation, using special pictures and other objects: "Walk by that table on which I have put some very familiar things and some pictures. Then without looking back, go to your seat, pick up paper and pencil and see how many things you can recall and list for me." (Pictures from Bible stories, names of characters or places can be written on blank cards and used on such a table.)

(e) "Stand exactly opposite a partner." (This exercise is to be done in pairs.) "We will call this line "A" and the others "B." Look over your partner very carefully — his hair, eyes, clothing — everything. In a moment I shall ask the "A" group to turn around, eyes closed. Each of the "B" group members will change some small thing about his appearance. The "A's" will now turn back and in two minutes each will try to discover what change has taken place in your partner's appearance." (The positions will be reversed the second time; the "B" group will turn around and the "A" group will make a change.) The same kind of exercise will work well, if the "A's" will make a simple pattern of gestures, perhaps four. The "B's" will then try to repeat the gestures exactly.

Listening

Brian Way, a British authority on child drama, believes that one should approach looking and listening exercises from the point of view of three different levels of attention: 1) intimate and personal (listening to one's own breathing); 2) close to one's immediate environment (sounds in the same room); and 3) in the world outside the immediate environment (distant sounds and sights). For some teachers, this method of encouraging concentrated listening works very well. The author has found it a little too abstract and demanding for the younger children. It is, however, a splendid approach for teenagers. The following exercises have proved very successful:

(a) The class will listen to several sounds made by the teacher, and try to repeat them in the same order.

(b) The teacher may clap a specific rhythm pattern or beat it on a drum. The children will try to repeat it by clapping or walking to it.

(c) With eyes closed, the children will listen to three different sounds made by the teacher or another student. Individual students may guess how these sounds were made. Examples, the sound made by hitting two pieces of metal together, striking an empty glass with a pencil, tapping the blackboard with the tip of a ruler.

Touching

(These exercises are often more effective if practiced with closed eyes.)

(a) The teacher sits with the children in a big circle on the floor. He will pass around several different objects, one at a time. Each child will feel the article carefully before sending it along. As it reaches the last child, one or all may be asked to describe it in detail.

(b) Have the children recall touch responses. Ask questions like: "What have you touched that makes you shiver?" "What have you touched that makes you feel comfortable, or afraid, or pain?"

(c) They may recall textures as they reply to these questions: "What can your feet touch that is smooth, soft, hard, rough, warm?"

(d) Ask the children to touch someone near them for one of the following reasons:

    (1) — to call his attention to something or someone;

    (2) — to hurry him along;

    (3) — to show him tenderness, sympathy, compassion.

SMELLING

(a) The children might imagine that they are arranging some very fragrant carnations or gardenias in a vase;

(b) or opening several imaginary bottles of perfume and after each one, decide which they like best;

(c) or walking around an old market place where, on one side, a fish merchant is exhibiting his early morning catch, on another the florist is filling his stand with fragrant flowers, and on a third, the baker is loading his outdoor counter with freshly made cakes and buns. (The teacher will indicate the placement of each stall; the children, as a group may wander about the market place at will, reacting to each merchant's wares as they approach them.)

TASTING

(a) Have the children close their eyes and imagine they are tasting April Fool candy. The first piece tastes like sour lemon; the second, like hot pepper; and the third is very bitter.

(b) Ask them to recall the taste of something they like very much; try the same thing with something they dislike.

(c) They might imagine that they are passing by three tables. On each is a bowl of what looks like delicious chocolate pudding (or some other popular dessert). Some little wooden spoons lie beside each bowl. Have them try the first bowl; it is very unpleasant, sour or bitter. The second bowl is so hot that it burns your mouth; the third bowl is smooth and delicious. (This exercise is done with a group of five or six, one at a time.)

Often one idea or question will motivate many children to creativity. The following "sense" question inspired a complete lesson. The teacher said: "Let's close our eyes and imagine that we smell smoke. Can you tell me where it comes from? Open your eyes now. What do you see?" After a moment, ideas come tumbling out in quick succession. "There's a pile of leaves burning in our back field!" "The smoke's coming out of the oven. Mother's on the phone and she forgot her cookies!" "It's the smoke from Grandfather's cigar. He's here on a surprise visit and I'm glad." These ideas, derived from the imaginary smell of smoke, provided the basis for some fine pantomime situations.

At the risk of being repetitive, let me emphasize again the importance of providing many opportunities for sharpening the senses. As children begin to respond naturally to imaginary stimuli, they will become more sensitive, aware, caring individuals, reaching out freely to motivate responsiveness in others.

Throughout the sessions devoted to sense and mood exercises, the teacher must constantly emphasize the importance of the second "key" —THINK THE THOUGHTS OF THE PERSON YOU'RE PRETENDING TO BE! The following story will exemplify the importance of the thought process. "Look, there comes Janice, my little two-year-old

sister, limping up the path, crying because she fell and scratched her knee. Poor thing! Let's imagine each of us in this circle sees a little Janice coming toward us . . . " Several of the group may fail to reach out sympathetic arms or may respond almost mechanically. During the evaluation period, the tactful, observant teacher asks: "What were you thinking when you saw Janice, Mary?" Mary seems unable to find a reply. Finally, she says: "I guess I thought she had fallen and I wondered whether I should help her . . . " The wise teacher will stop this meandering and suggest: "Mary, the thoughts in your head are like words you might say to yourself. You know what it feels like to talk to yourself, don't you? Well . . . these are thoughts! Now, pretend you see little Janice approaching and talk to yourself out loud." Almost at once, ideas are crystallized. Mary says: "Oh . . . poor Janice! Your knee is bleeding. Come here, Janice, let me fix it, you poor little thing! There, don't cry any more!" As she speaks this time, Mary moves forward, leans down and tenderly lifts up an imaginary Janice. Her natural, spontaneous thoughts have made the scene come alive!

This kind of experience provides an opportunity for the teacher to make a very important observation: A person must never tell his body what to do. His thoughts will motivate movement that is believable and real. Never must he say to himself: "Now I must act afraid, or show that I am angry." This kind of thinking produces artificial, awkward movement patterns which are often ludicrous.

Early in this stage of the project, the teacher should explain differences in personal reactions. Everyone doesn't think in exactly the same word pattern when he is angry, afraid or sad, nor does everybody react to thought patterns with the same kind of movement. Each child must be assured that as long as his responses are honest and truthful, motivated by his character's thoughts, they will be sincere and believable. This is an appropriate time to note that some people's bodies and faces respond to emotions in small ways because they have been conditioned to conceal their feelings. It is wise to explain how important it is for all of us to learn to communicate our thoughts and feelings. One might say: "How can Mother help you when you're in trouble, comfort you when you're sad, if you don't let her know how you feel and what you're thinking?" or "How can parents and friends know when we are happy, or sad, or afraid? And if they don't know, how can they share our joys or sorrows?" One is deepening Christian education principles when one helps children to build free, warm human relationships. Reuel Howe stresses this point when he says: " . . . we awaken trust not by the use of the language of words alone, but by the use of another language . . . much more basic, the language of relationship, the language of trust and love."

Beginning work in the area of Mood Pantomime seems to fall naturally into three divisions:

(1) Exercises designed to sharpen the senses (to which we have already referred).

(2) The playing of situations controlled by one dominant mood, as one's self.

(3) Playing a situation, controlled by a single mood, as a completely different personality. Again, as in the earlier steps, the first assignments should be appropriate for group playing.

If necessary, a portion of the available space could be allotted to each child to avoid confusion. Plenty of time should be spent on a discussion of the exercise before it is attempted. All questions about content, the appearance of the scene itself, the exact point at which the playing begins, should be brought up and answered. Children can only feel secure if they have a clear understanding of every detail. Since there is no dramatic form (beginning, middle and end) in a mood pantomime exercise, the teacher is still responsible for beginning and ending it, unless the material itself provides a natural closing. For example, in the following situation, no technique for ending the action is necessary; the placement of those involved will automatically provide the conclusion:

"You have just left school to walk home. The school doors are over there, against the left wall (teacher indicates). It will be hard to face Mother this afternoon for in your book bag is a most disappointing report card. You have dropped down to a "C" in History and English; what's more you know it is your fault. You spent too much time on TV this semester, were late turning in two book reports and had a bad mark on a History exam. You are feeling guilty and ashamed as you reach your front door. The right wall, over there, (teacher indicates) is home. When you reach there, the scene is over."

By contrast, the scene to follow implies no beginning or ending, so the teacher must find some way to start and finish the action pattern:

"You've been working for almost an hour on one set of mathematic problems which are terribly difficult for you. You have tried and tried, unsuccessfully, to come up with a plausible answer to even one of them. It's late, and you're discouraged and exhausted. What's to be done?"

After discussing the situation, how one feels, and what thoughts might come in such a predicament, six children will be selected (if space permits) and asked to take their chairs and put them in the open space. Each will imagine a desk or table cluttered with books and papers in front of him. When everyone is settled, the teacher might say:

"Perhaps, when you're just so angry and tired you can't go on any longer, you could close your book, in disgust, and go downstairs to get a glass of milk."

This will give them a thought which will motivate them to leave the acting area and go back to join the rest of the group. Each child will decide for himself how long to spend on his homework efforts. Although this will mean that each will return to his place at a different time, this will not be confusing because the wise teacher will already have explained that since everyone's thought patterns are different, they would seldom finish the same pantomime at exactly the same time.

Children can play the following situations as themselves or as another character. For example, in the first trial of the first exercise, a little girl might exercise her own reactions to the circumstance. The second time, she might pretend that she is a very poor child who has only one dress fit to wear.

For Ages Eight To Ten

1. Come in to show Mother the rip in your new dress, made when you caught it in a rough board on the neighbor's fence.

2. You are returning to your summer cabin in the mountains from a service in the little country church. There has been a sudden drenching rainstorm, so you must hunt for the high, dry spots in the field as you cross to get in your car.

3. You must have lost your new ring in a field where you were playing ball after the picnic lunch down by the river. Search and search in the high grass for this special ring which means so much to you. Grandma gave it to you. You realize you should not have worn it to a ball game!

4. You're sitting disconsolately by the window or pacing the room. It's pouring rain on Saturday, the day planned for a family beach outing. You've been looking forward to this day with such joy! It's to be your first outing after being ill for three weeks. And now, it's raining!

5. Grandfather, your favorite friend, has come from New York to visit you. It's his birthday. You've made him a little calendar and you're creeping down the hall to surprise him.

6. You went with Mother on an errand in the neighboring town. She has asked you to meet her on a specific corner after your visit to the zoo. You have been waiting here now, in the appointed spot, for half an hour. There is still no sign of Mother. It's getting dark, and you don't even have a dime for a phone call.

7. Your teacher, whom you like very much, is coming for dinner at your house. Mother has suggested that you pick and arrange the flowers. Let's pretend that it's almost time for the guest's arrival. Your flowers are lying on the kitchen table. The vase, filled with water, stands ready. You rush to arrange the flowers; there's not much time. Just as you place the last bud in the vase, you hear the car outside.

For Ages Eleven To Thirteen

1. Walk home from school after having had a serious argument with a very good friend; you feel miserable.

2. You are waiting at the airport for a much-loved aunt or uncle who has been living abroad for many years. The plane is late, but is due at any moment now. It's exciting!

3. Pick up the pieces of a valuable vase which your new puppy has just knocked to the floor by bumping the table. You realize this is your fault because you should not have been playing ball with him in the living room.

4. You've been shopping and your arms are full of bundles. You are trying to get across a crowded street where the traffic is heavy.

5. It's a very windy day. You're trying to set up the table in the patio for a special outdoor supper party. You simply cannot make that table cloth lie down!

6. You are sitting in front of a mirror, trying on a beautiful necklace you have just received for your birthday. It is something you have been wanting for months!

7. You are trying to finish a dessert at your friend's dinner table. It is dreadfully sour and you can hardly swallow another mouthful. You're trying hard not to let your friend and her family know how you feel.

8. You are reading a mystery story one evening as you sit alone in your aunt's house in the country. It's an old house, and because there's a high wind, there are strange rattles and noises everywhere. Shutters bang occasionally; the wind in the chimney has an almost human sound. It is an uncomfortable feeling! If only the family would come home soon!

5

Creative Drama
Three More Steps

When the time comes to progress to CHANGE-OF-MOOD pantomime, the transition will be made from dramatic play to DRAMA. So
far, there has been no suggestion of plot in the exercises, no starting
point, and few limitations of time set by the form of the material. The
bridge, however, is a natural one. In life, one may feel joy at good news
in the morning and as quickly sink into disappointment upon discovering that it was false. Before long, a chance may come to offer a real
service to a friend in need. The momentary sadness disappears. One's
average day is, in fact, a series of responses to different stimuli, and
behavior is motivated by many changes of mood.

THE FOURTH STEP —
CHANGE-OF-MOOD PANTOMIME

The first few classes devoted to this practice should use relatively
simple material involving no more than one mood change. Some of
the MOOD PANTOMIME material can easily be supplemented for
this purpose. This is a real time saver, because the situations and
characters are already familiar and need little introductory
discussions. For example, the child searching for the lost ring in the
field can find it. The girl attempting to lay the cloth on the picnic table
in the high wind can imagine it blown out of her hands and into a
mud puddle. While waiting at the airport for the favorite aunt's
arrival, the child may hear it announced that because of storms, the
plane must land in another city.

It is still best to work in groups of five or six; each child will be
playing his own situation, in his own way, as a single individual.
Obviously, every participant's ending would come at a different time;
again, it is wise to remind the children that each must remain in his
own acting area until all have completed the exercise. Otherwise, a
child, walking across the room to his seat, may completely block out
the picture or thought pattern of his neighbor who has not finished.

As facility and concentration grow, more complex situations may
be attempted, involving two or more changes of mood. By this time, it

is obvious that most of the improvisations are taking dramatic form. There is a beginning, a climactic moment, and a solution or denouement. A conflict is presented, a problem to be solved; some difficulty which stands in the way of this solution must be overcome. This, indeed, is DRAMA.

Some of the class will now be ready to attempt simple dramatizations which require working together as a related group of friends or family members. This is a new and far more challenging experience than working as individuals, not relating to one another in any way. In that kind of creative activity, the only kind practiced so far, each child has responded to his own thought patterns, working entirely individually. Now his reactions to another's feelings, when playing in a related group situation, influence his expression. He must readjust his thoughts and actions as he works in a group playing together as a group.

The teacher, too, has a new problem as he approaches this stage of the project. Since each change of mood may be motivated by a *sound* or *sight* to which all must respond at once, the cue for the change must be given by the teacher. For example: several members of the family might be reading, in the living room of Aunt Sally's big country house on a windy evening (see Mood Pantomime #8). Even the natural creaking noises in an old house are a bit frightening. Suddenly, there's a different sound, heard by everyone — the sound of footsteps on the brick path and then on the porch. Several of the group may cling together for comfort; another one may run to the window to look out. The latter, greatly relieved to see Aunt Sally returning with her guest, beckons to the others to come to the window. There is general relief and relaxation of tension as they all run off to greet Aunt Sally. In this story, it is vitally important for *all* the children to hear the sound which motivated the apprehension, at exactly the same time. It will be the teacher's responsibility to invent the sound cue and give it at an appropriate time. He will explain in the beginning, as he discusses the playing of the story, exactly what the cue will be — perhaps a clapping of hands or a tapping of his foot on the floor. The group will then expect the sound, and there will be no difficulty imagining it to be the menacing footsteps on the brick path. Were the same exercise to be done in a group, in which each child is acting individually and has no relationship to any other, each one could hear the footsteps when he wished, react when he wished and finish the scene in his own time. Another suggestion may be helpful to the teacher who is attempting this change-of-mood group pantomime. His material must be selected and prepared with great care. After he tells the story, a detailed discussion of the situation, a description of the scene, and a clear explanation of exactly where the playing begins, are essential. Asking the children key questions is often the best way to clarify the project. The discussion preparatory to playing the scene described above might go like this:

Teacher: What are some of your thoughts as you sit there reading your mystery story at Aunt Sally's that windy night?

Child 1: Gee . . . that's a funny sound! I don't like it.

Child 2: I might think "That sounds like somebody moaning — it's almost human!"

Child 3: How long do we have to stay here alone, I wonder?

Child 4: Gee! This is a spooky place!

Teacher: Fine! These are fine thoughts! I would have the same, I think. And what thoughts do we have as we hear the footsteps?

Child 1: Hey! What's that? I heard something.

Child 2: It's footsteps. Somebody's coming up the walk.

Child 3: I'm scared. Let's hide.

Child 4: I'm going to look and see who it is.

Teacher: Good. That's great. And it's true some of us would be more frightened than others. Surely someone would suggest that it would be more sensible to see who was coming. Shall we decide who, in each group, will be the brave one?

It is agreed that in each of the four groups doing this scene, one child is selected who will be most afraid or most brave, etc. The discussion will include enough questions to assure the teacher that every detail of the assignment is clear and everyone feels comfortable and ready to play. They must know precisely where the window is, the porch, the door to the room, etc.

To summarize:

(1) The material must be appropriate, interesting and within the comprehension of the group participating.

(2) It must be dramatic in form, with a beginning or initial incident, a story line rising to a climax and a satisfactory ending.

(3) Incidents concerning sound human relationships, which provide opportunities for discussion of right attitudes and philosophies should take preference.

(4) Bringing the story to life by telling it vividly and dramatically will influence the quality and sincerity of the playing.

(5) A detailed question period and discussion to clarify any blurred points is essential. Planning for individual characterizations and sound cues comes at this time.

For Ages Eight To Ten

The following exercises will be done by the children acting as individuals:*

(1) Come in from school, expecting an invitation to your friend's big party. It should have come in today's mail. Look through the letters on the table. There is nothing for you. You are very disappointed.

(2) Mother has asked you to finish putting the books back on the shelf in the living room; your aunt, who is coming for a visit, is due any moment. You're hurrying with the task because you are anxious to go outside to play. As usual when we're too hasty, something always seems to go wrong. This time, you accidentally hit the top edge of the bookcase and knock a lovely little vase to the floor. You're terribly worried as you pick it up, knowing how Mother cherishes it. Examine it carefully. Thank goodness! It's not broken. Put it back, along with the last book and go off, thankful that you were so fortunate.

(3) One Friday afternoon in spring, you come home from school, hot and tired. It's been a very long day and much too warm for this time of the year! You discover a note from Mother on the table near the door. It reads: "I've gone to the store for some supplies. Get your things together quickly. We're off to the beach for the weekend." Overjoyed, you dash off upstairs to pack.

The following situations will work well for groups:

(1) You, your sister and a friend have been playing outside and decide to take a rest. Come in through the kitchen door.

---

*In these exercises each child acts out the scene individually. The teacher should, however, have several children do the exercise simultaneously, each giving it his own unique interpretation but without any interaction among the participants. If the child does the exercise all by himself, he might become inhibited and self-conscious.

There, on the table, are two plates of your favorite cookies. Mother has just baked them for guests who are coming for tea. You are so dying for one — just one. All of you are about to snatch one. Then, somehow you resist the temptation. Start into the living room, when suddenly you hear Mother calling from upstairs: "Children, help yourselves to the

cookies. I have many more than I need." Delighted with the news, you run back, each one takes a cookie or two and then goes off to the living room, munching happily.

(2) You are down at the seashore playing in the sand. The sun is shining brightly and there is a fine breeze. You are so interested in the big fort that four of you are building that you don't even notice the gathering clouds and the distant sound of thunder. Then suddenly a few raindrops fall and almost before you can realize the approach of a big storm, the sky seems to open. Gather up your sweaters, buckets and towels and run for shelter. The closest protection is a lifeguards' boat which is beached and turned on its side. There is just enough room for four of you. Huddle together there until the worst of the rain is over.

The following exercises should be done as individuals:

(1) You are about to enter a movie for which a friend had bought your ticket. As you approach the attendant, reach into your jacket pocket for your ticket; it is *not there.* Suddenly you think of your wallet; you may have put it in there for safekeeping. Look for it. Yes! Thank goodness! There it is.

(2) You have been working for ages on a difficult mathematical problem. It has you completely baffled. Suddenly a new thought comes to you; you decide to try a different approach. As you realize that it is working, you are delighted and finish the addition without any more trouble. Close your book, happily.

(3) You are waiting outside a bakery, enjoying a bag of fresh buns. Your mother has said she will meet you here. Suddenly you notice a little girl, about your age, longingly looking into the bake shop window. She is very thin and dressed in old clothes. She, too, must be waiting for someone. You feel so sorry for her. Finally you get the courage to offer her a bun. She takes it, hesitatingly. She is so grateful and from the way she devours it you know how little she must have had to eat today. Her name is called soon and she runs off to meet her father, waving to you in gratitude as she goes down the street. (This exercise can be done by one child with an imaginary poor little girl, or with two children.)

(4) You are a little late leaving school today because you had some questions you needed the teacher to answer. As you come out the school door you see the bus which is to take you home stopping at the corner. Worried that the driver may not see you, wave to him to attract his attention. He responds, puts on the brakes and opens the bus door for you to get in!

The following exercises are to be done by groups:

(1) (Pairs of children are suggested here.) You are twins, and it's your birthday. You are returning from school, very miserable because nobody has remembered your birthday. There was not even a card on the breakfast table this morning. Since Mother is in the hospital, you were sure that Daddy would make a special effort to greet you. Instead, he left early. You feel as though everyone has forgotten you and you're thinking some very unkind thoughts about Daddy. As you arrive at

your own gate and start up the path, you both notice a basket on the doorstep. What can this be? You hurry up to investigate and discover a card on the top containing both your names. It reads, "Happy birthday you two! Sorry to be late with this. But you see, I didn't forget after all. Love, Dad." And at that moment, you feel pretty ashamed of those thoughts you had about your Dad! Suddenly, you hear a tiny whining sound coming from inside the basket. One of you lifts the top; there inside, much to your delight, is a puppy, the very one you had seen last week at the pet shop and wanted so much. (This kind of situation offers an excellent opportunity for discussion of self-pity, unjust criticism and the like.)

(2) Three children meet with their little banks to decide what they will buy for Mother's birthday. They have been baby-sitting, running errands, and trying very hard to save enough to get the bedroom slippers she wants and needs so badly. Each dumps his or her bag on the rug. As they count together, silently, they realize that the total is fifty cents short. And Mother's birthday is only two days away! Then suddenly, one shakes her bank extra hard; she seems to hear something rattling inside. Out comes the much-needed fifty cents! Thankfully, they gather up the money and go off to the store.

(3) You and your sisters are staying by a lovely lake, visiting your cousin's home during the summer holiday. Come out on Saturday morning with your towels all ready to go swimming. You've had three days of rain and cold, sharp winds. This morning you woke up to welcome sunshine. As you get to the porch steps, you realize that the wind has blown down three of your Aunt Polly's prize plants. They are lying on the ground and several of the pots are broken. What will you do? How do you feel? Perhaps you so want that swim that you will ignore what you see and dash on. Perhaps one of you will go on to the lake and the others will stay to pick up the plants and carry them to the garden house. (Divide the class into several groups of three. Let them have a few minutes to discuss the scene quietly, decide how they will end the change-of-mood exercise. Each child may determine what his character reactions will be. This material offers ample opportunity for meaningful discussion of joy in service.)

(4) You are walking in the woods with some friends, exploring this beautiful mountain spot where you are visiting. Your little puppy, Tippy, has been running along with you dashing here and there deep in the forest. Suddenly you all hear a sharp cry. The whimpering which follows it must come from Tippy. Look around and finally place the sound, then run off in that direction. There in some underbrush lies Tippy. He was trying to get under an old fence and a loose board fell off, pinning him under it. One of the children helps lift the board. Another releases Tippy, who is unhurt, and runs off once more on his adventures. The children follow him, relieved and happy.

THE FIFTH STEP — BEGINNING TO USE DIALOGUE

By this time, the atmosphere is probably relaxed, warm and friendly; children are beginning to feel secure and free in expressing thoughts and feelings; concentration and creative interaction are noticeably improved. It is time to take the next and sometimes difficult step — communicating with words. Although the transition to dialogue is a natural one, work with spoken improvisations does present some new problems. Sometimes the first sound of one's own voice causes a shock, and may even bring back some of the early inhibitions. Another stumbling block is the limited vocabulary of most children. What they find easy to say with their bodies becomes a real dilemma when words are required. This is especially true of children whose speech has constantly been corrected at home or at school. They may have become so self-conscious in this area that they almost wait to be told what to say and how to say it. The teacher who has been forewarned about this problem should not be discouraged by a temporary setback. He must, however, remember to require very little of these children at the outset in order not to give any of them a sense of failure or inadequacy.

It may be helpful to discuss once more the two "keys" to creative dramatization:

(1) Make a picture in your mind of the place and the things involved in the story;

(2) Think the thoughts of the character you are playing, never your own thoughts.

It is important to point out the relationship of thoughts and feelings to the pitch, quality and inflection of the voice. Since they have already been made aware of how their thoughts and feelings change their body movements, the effect on their speech should seem reasonable and they can be convinced by a simple demonstration. The teacher might imagine he is opening a box, a surprise birthday gift, and say, "A present! How delightful, and just what I wanted, too!" Then he may open another similar box for his birthday (which by chance falls on April 1). This time he finds the box empty except for a card which he will read: "April Fool — but Happy Birthday anyway!" His voice, in the second case, will register disappointment and perhaps some resentment.

A third explanation, which should help all children with their first dialogue efforts, concerns the importance of the senses as motivators for every change of thought and feeling. One hears (sees, smells, touches or tastes), then one thinks, and *then* one speaks. The need for this three-step procedure can be easily proven by a simple exercise. Line up four or five children and ask them to pass along an imaginary hall to the imaginary door of the bedroom which they left this morning. Place two chairs about three feet apart to represent the doorway. The door stands open. Suggest that something has happened since morning to change the appearance of this room. As each child reaches his door, he will see the change (what has occurred in each room is up to the individual to decide). He will think whatever the sight might call for, and then speak, using only a simple exclamation such as "Well!" "Goodness," or "Oh." The first might see some water color paint spilled on the new white rug because little sister has been careless. Another might see a big box tied up with bright ribbon. A third might see new curtains on the windows. It will seem obvious, as the children try this exercise, that the class can only correctly guess the motivation for speech, from the single word or two, if the player has followed the three-step procedure: 1) look, 2) think, 3) speak.

The following improvisation, which gives convincing proof of the effect of thoughts and feelings on the voice quality, may be helpful. Ask a child to make two separate entrances into the living room where Mother is sitting, sewing. Each time she will use the same phrase, but each time under completely different circumstances. The first time, the child has just received a new dress from her Aunt Grace. It is beautiful and has arrived just in time for her birthday. She says: "Mother, look at my new dress." Her voice is full of joy. The second time, the child runs in from a party she has been attending in the neighbor's garden. The dog has jumped up to greet her and has torn her delicate, lace-trimmed party dress. This time she says: "Mother, look at my new dress!" Her voice is full of tears. She is distressed at the unavoidable accident.

The teacher must remember that he is now asking for solo performances for the first time. The pantomime exercises done previously have used first large groups and then small groups. Work in dialogue requires just the opposite; groups of two or three are best at the outset. If improvisations are attempted with five or more in the beginning, the results may be chaotic. Everyone may speak at once, or there may be no response at all, for each one often waits for another to begin.

Other simple situations which require only one word or phrase, like the examples mentioned above, include: AT LAST! MINE! HELLO! GONE! WAIT! The children might select one from this list (and there are many others equally appropriate), and they will be asked to imagine specific circumstances in which the word might be spoken. As each says his chosen word, the rest of the class might guess how the speaker feels and what circumstances motivated the exclamation. This is an excellent way to prove the premise discussed at the beginning — that speech is a three-step procedure, and if it is to be believable, there will always be a definite situation and a reason for the feeling involved.

After a few hours spent on these introductory exercises, most of the class will be ready to attempt some very simple scenes in which two or three characters appear. Such scenes should require only a few spoken words. Some of the change-of-mood pantomime material, already used, may be easily adapted for this purpose. Since these scenes have already been discussed by the group, the characters are old friends and the settings are familiar. Take for example Exercise #1 in those suggested for groups of eight-to-ten-year-olds, appearing on page 55. The teacher might recall it this way: "Remember the story we played, in pantomime, about the little girl, whom we'll call Jean, and her sister and a friend, coming in on a Saturday afternoon and finding a tempting plate of Mother's cookies, just freshly baked? What do you think they might be talking about as they discovered them?" The replies would go something like this: "Oh, boy, am I hungry!" "Look at those marvelous cookies, dozens of them!" "And do they smell good!" "Let's try a couple, couldn't we, Jean?" And Jean might reply: "Well, Mommy's going to have some ladies meeting here for tea. I really don't think we should!" More suggestions might come, some of them expressing sound arguments for taking just one or two that wouldn't be missed. "Now, do you remember," the teacher will continue, "that Mother calls from upstairs and offers us all we want. That settles everything. We thank her and dash out with our mouths full and pockets bulging!"

Very little dialogue is really needed here. What *is* needed is simple and obvious. The teacher, or another student, would give Mother's lines from "upstairs." Timing for this interruption is important; that is, deciding exactly when Mother will speak. This kind of exercise provides an excellent opportunity for the discussion of temptation and how hard it is, when you're so hungry, to remember about Mother's guests and how difficult it is to do the right thing under similar circumstances. The wise leader will find a way, during this talk, to point out the fact that often, if one *can* resist temptation, things work out for the best anyway, as they did in the story just told. The children's rewards were forthcoming — pockets full of cookies!

Three or four groups of three would be selected to play the same scene. The kitchen playing space would be marked off, the door, and the table for the cookies indicated; every detail of the setting would be clarified. The first group would try the improvisation and a lively discussion would follow. What did we believe? Did we really see who was most tempted to take a cookie? Did we see relief and joy when Mother spoke? These and other questions are likely to pull everyone into the discussion; suggestions may even come for ideas which can be added to the dialogue. The second and third groups will then try their interpretations; probably vocabulary and fluency will increase noticeably. It is wise for the teacher to remember that he must set the tone for each critique period by beginning with an affirmative remark such as, "Wasn't the delight on those faces lovely when they discovered the cookies? I could almost smell them myself!" Children relax and feel comfortable in an atmosphere of acceptance, they are more secure when they feel they have succeeded. It is in this kind of atmosphere that they can be free enough to accept constructive criticism, and this is when growth takes place. According to Arthur Jersild, the psychologist, "the satisfaction that a child derives from being able to do something well is an important factor in his growing conception of himself." The affirmative comment from the teacher also sets a good example for the observing children. They will be encouraged to make constructive, helpful suggestions rather than resort to cruel, inappropriate criticism.

Often in a small group dialogue scene, there is a sound which every participant must hear at once. In the second exercise for the eight-to-ten-year-old group, on page 55, the children were happily playing on the beach when there was a sharp roll of thunder. Certainly they must all hear the imaginary thunder at the same time if the dialogue is to turn, at once, to seeking shelter from the storm. In this case, the teacher must be prepared to give the sound cue as he did during the work in pantomime. He should explain what the sound of the cue will be, drum beats, hand claps, or whatever seems most appropriate. This will prevent the children's thought patterns from being sharply broken by a strange, unexpected noise. In some stories, it is possible to give the responsibility for a special cue to a single child. For example, if children are preparing a surprise birthday party for Mother and she arrives unexpectedly ahead of time, one can be designated to go to the window at a certain time and see Mother's car in the driveway. This will motivate the action to follow and the teacher need not be called upon to give any sound cue.

As the class becomes more facile in dialogue improvisation, the material selected may present more challenges and make more demands upon the imagination. It is interesting sometimes to offer a beginning or ending of a story, leaving its completion to the group involved. Here is an example: One cool night in fall, two sisters (or brothers) and their two weekend guests went to the movies with neighbors. They have been given a door key because Mother and Father, who have gone off for dinner, fear they may not be home when the children return. The four come up the walk, chattering happily about the film. Suddenly, Dotty, who has been entrusted with the key, cries: "The key's gone! I've lost it!" What can they do? How might they solve the problem?

There are many ways of suggesting ideas for improvised scenes. Sometimes a place — an airport, an attic, a garden — or an article such as a ring, a box, a letter, will provoke imaginative thinking. A combination of these, with a mood added, will often provide material for an interesting improvisation. The teacher may prepare three envelopes; the first will contain slips of paper, each displaying the name of an object such as a ring, box, book, or vase; the slips in the second envelope will each mention a single mood or feeling such as fear, anger, joy, hate; each slip in the third envelope will suggest a place, perhaps the cellar, garden, hotel, or store. Groups of three or four children are selected. A child from each group will take a slip from each envelope. He will then go off with his group members to a quiet spot in the room where they can pool their ideas for the next five minutes and create a scene using the material drawn from the envelopes. Each group will then play its scene, announcing the given ideas on which it was built. The evaluation and discussion will concern the believability of the characters as well as the skill in using the foundation material.

Let us take a moment now to consider the remarkable growth potential, inherent in this free work in small groups, where individual opinions are freely given, exchanged, reordered and utilized. Regina Wieman labels this process *creative interaction* which she defines this way: ". . . when we, with others, mutually, freely and honestly express ourselves in work and play . . . there ensues a quickening . . . challenging, inspiring interplay. This results in an increase of sensitivity and responsiveness . . . each participant can see his own interests and ways in a new light. The old self can never be quite the same again. It has been recreated by intercommunicating with other persons . . . we shall refer to all this reciprocating stimulation and responsiveness, as *creative interaction* . . . it is that manifestation of God which is always going on in the family and within which its members can most readily work. We call this interaction creative, because wherever it occurs, it reorganizes the situation so that there is more for each to appreciate and each person is so transformed that he can appreciate more." As children express their thoughts, and discuss ways of utilizing the suggestions offered, they are simultaneously deepening their understanding of themselves and their peers. Close human relationships grow during this free interchange. Mrs. Wieman uses the term "valuings" to describe this situation. This word is aptly chosen, for it refers to the value an individual places upon his interests, ambitions, prejudices, attitudes, loves and hates. As one expresses his own valuings and exchanges them with another, creative interaction occurs. The valuings of both are enriched.

This part of our creative drama work, the group development of dialogue improvisations, offers a unique opportunity for individual growth in sympathy, compassion and the ability to express emotions. Let us not be afraid of using material which encourages strong emotional response. If we fail in this respect, we may justify the accusation often hurled at the kind school which, as someone said recently, "is more concerned with a child's fractured limb than with his fractured feelings." If a youngster is to acquire emotional health, he must be allowed to show and examine his feelings, and be helped to understand himself and his behavior in a realistic way. When we over-emphasize academic training and the outward forms of social conformity, children's emotional development is impaired. Dr. George Brain, for a short time Superintendent of Public Instruction in Baltimore, Maryland, said on this subject, ". . . the area of human relationships is one of the most important in determining the successes which individuals and nations experience in the course of their history. . . . Man's actions are influenced by and reflect his emotional condition. . . . If society is to be served, it is essential that every child be helped by Baltimore schools to develop emotional maturity."

An appropriate time for the discussion of the importance of good, believable and expressive speech patterns is during this work with dialogue. Although the focus is always on the relationship between thought, feeling and speech, emphasizing the fact that convincing, meaningful speech comes from within, occasions may arise when the children themselves will sense a need for improvement. Such an opportunity came one day when a little girl asked: "How can I make the queen sound more royal? I don't know how to make a smooth, silvery queen's voice!" She was asking for help! This is the moment for the teacher to offer some simple suggestions for avoiding nasality, developing resonance, and pronouncing final consonants. Only when the children feel a need for improving speech in order to portray character more effectively, will they really work at it. When children feel confident that they can spontaneously find words to express their ideas and that their thoughts add something worthwhile to a dialogue scene; only then should we work toward developing clearer and more fluent speech patterns.

One amusing set of verses, although based on a completely impossible and fantastic situation, has provided me with successful practice in the vowel sounds: E, O, I, OO.

The lines are:

1. Whee! We're free! (the long "e" sound)
2. Oh! The snow! (the long "o" sound)
3. Hi! Let's fly! (the long "i" sound)
4. OO! He flew! (the long "oo" sound)

An appropriate story sequence is difficult to imagine at a glance. It goes this way: Two friends, who are usually very restricted and seldom allowed to seek adventure, finally run off to explore a mysterious land. At the opening of the scene, one has wandered off and is standing on a high cliff. The other, (who speaks), is down in the valley, standing amid heaps of brightly colored leaves. He tosses an armful above his head in glee, rejoicing in his new-found freedom, saying, "Whee! We're free!" As he looks down, presumably to gather up some more leaves, he stops suddenly, shocked. Some magic has turned the beautiful leaves to snow. He moans in disappointment, "Oh! It's snow!" Then hearing his friend's whistle from the cliff above, he looks up, waves and cries jokingly, "Hi! Let's fly!" Much to his amazement, his friend takes him seriously and, assisted by pure magic, he takes off across the sky like a kite. In absolute awe and amazement, the first child watches the performance until his friend is out of sight, saying, "OOOO! He flew!" This kind of speech exercise is eminently successful, because above all, it is great fun! At the same time, the most important vowel sounds are practiced. The possibilities for originating other similar exercises are infinite.

For Ages Eight To Ten

Several of the exercises already suggested for change-of-mood pantomimes can be readily adapted for simple dialogue (see pages 54 and 55).

1. Come home from school with a friend who has asked to borrow one of your books. You are talking as you enter the house about school, or the book, and go directly to the table where the mail is usually placed. You are expecting an invitation to a friend's party. Some other children have already received theirs, so you are hopeful. Unfortunately, there is no letter addressed to you. You can hardly help showing your disappointment and explaining it to your friend

who tries to encourage you with a remark about slow mail service. Suddenly your mother calls from upstairs to say that she has put your mail on the desk in your room. Delighted, you both run off to see whether the coveted invitation has arrived.

2. The exercise about the broken vase will work very well with dialogue if we imagine that Mother, hearing the crash of the vase, came running in to see what had occurred. Here we have a dramatic dialogue potential. She would pick up the vase very worried and then to her delight, find that it did not break. Of course your instant apology is sincere, but Mother cannot refrain from giving you some much-needed advice about "haste makes waste."

3. In this pantomime, you come home on a hot Friday afternoon to learn that a beach weekend has been planned. It can become a successful dialogue exercise if your sister (or brother) comes home with you, and when you enter you discover the note on the table and read it aloud. The ensuing conversation will be filled with exciting plans for the anticipated journey.

4. Many ideas can be drawn from biblical material. A lively dialogue will surely emerge if you imagine an occasion when two little Egyptian children, who are playing down by the river, come across the baby Moses hidden in the cradle of rushes. One might hear the crying child and follow the sound to discover the infant. Then, after a little conversation, one might decide to go tell someone at the palace, and the others offer to stay and comfort the baby.

Some of the suggestions for this age group's change-of-mood pantomimes starting on page 56 can also be used as basic material for dialogue exercises.

1. The situation marked No. 2 which concerns the baffling mathematics problem, will work very well. Your friend next door, who has also been having some homework difficulty, but has the answer to the mathematics problem, comes in to look at your work and points out your mistake. Delighted, you finish and both of you go off for a bike ride.

2. The situation already described on page 56 about enjoying the delicious fresh buns works well with dialogue, because the little poor child who is mentioned in the story can become part of an interesting conversation which can develop quite naturally.

3. The story of the twins' forgotten birthday on pages 56 and 57 also makes the basis for a natural dialogue scene. The two children can be commiserating with one another over the forgotten birthday in this manner: "Even Daddy forgot . . . he went off early and didn't even leave us a card." When they discover the basket on the doorstep and hear the whine of the puppy they so much wanted, their joy knows no bounds! They feel a little remorseful over the unkind thoughts they harbored about Daddy.

4. Exercises 3 and 4 on pages 57 and 58 need almost no adjustment to prepare them for use with conversation.

5. Many situations from biblical material will serve as a basis for dialogue work. A telling of the Ruth and Naomi story, in dialogue form, will often inspire interesting improvisations. A simple plan follows: Ruth, Orpah, and Naomi are wearily travelling across country. Naomi's two sons, once husbands to the Moabite girls, Ruth and Orpah, have been killed.

NAOMI: Let us stop here and rest, my children. We have travelled far today.

ORPAH: Yes, dear Mother Naomi, you must indeed be weary.

RUTH: Wait until I put my robe down on the ground for you, Mother (*she does so, and Naomi sits*).

NAOMI: Thank you, daughter. You are both always so good and kind. For ten long years, you've been good wives to my sons and good daughters to their mother.

ORPAH: How could we have been otherwise, Mother, with such fine young men as Mahlon and Chilion for husbands?

NAOMI: Now they are gone, both of them, gone to their Father in Heaven! And we remain here, three lonely women! I fear I brought you more grief than joy when I took my little family to the land of Moab.

NAOMI: But I must return to my people in Bethlehem, and it is best that you return, each to your mother's house. May the Lord deal kindly with you as you have dealt with me.

RUTH: Nay, Mother. I will return with you to your people! (*Naomi urges them once more to go to their own land. Finally, Orpah agrees, asks for Naomi's blessing and leaves. But when she asks Ruth if she will accompany her, Ruth says that she cannot leave Naomi. When Naomi again urges Ruth to go, the latter replies with those beautiful, familiar words*):

RUTH: Entreat me not to leave thee, or to return from following after thee, for whither thou goest, I will go and where thou lodgest, I will lodge. Thy people shall be my people, and thy God, my God. Where thou diest, will I die and there will I be buried.

NAOMI: My heart is deeply touched, Ruth. I can scarcely find words to reply. If this is your wish, then so be it!

RUTH: It is my wish, Mother dear; so let us be on our way. (*She picks up the robe, puts her arms about Naomi, and they wander off together.*)

This arrangement of the Ruth narrative for telling can be used as a basis for the older children's improvisation. It is given here merely as an example of the way small biblical incidents can be treated. Another excellent situation, appropriate for boys, is an imaginary conversation which might have taken place between Saul, as a boy, and some of the sea captains from the Mediterranean who put in at the Tarsus docks. This could center around Saul's interest in travel, other peoples, and his love of the sea. This kind of scene can lay the groundwork for a deeper understanding of his missionary journeys after his conversion.

THE SIXTH STEP — PLAYING THE STORY

During the hours spent on simple dialogue improvisations, a sense of security in using speech will have developed. Hopefully, vocabulary will have increased and a subconscious awareness of the fundamentals of dramatic form is likely to have appeared. Many of the change-of-mood pantomimes, on which the longer improvisations were based, contained the essence of conflict: an initial incident, action rising to a climax, and a denouement. By this time, the young people progress from the natural, formless make-believe of dramatic play to the beginnings of drama. They have discovered for themselves which scenes are most fun to play and have certain characteristics in common. The wise teacher recognizes this fact. In selecting material for miniature story-playing, he will be sure that it always incorporates the following requirements. It should possess:

1. A strong appeal to the emotions, especially those of the particular group participating.
2. Action that moves and interests, and can be played in the facility available.
3. Adequate conflict expressed in a plot line, rising steadily to a climax.
4. A resolution which leads, without delay, to a satisfactory ending.
5. Characters that are true to life, understandable and believable.
6. Incidents which can be conveniently grouped into a few closely knit scenes.
7. A worthwhile theme, or central idea, which represents living truths that are essentially religious in nature.

Sources for interesting story ideas are many. Appropriate Bible stories, moments drawn from the biographies of real people or favorite characters from literature, all provide rich, workable material. Incidents which contain sound Christian attitudes are recommended. There is nothing that can arouse in a child the deep meaning of a spiritual truth like the presentation in words and action of a moving story exemplifying that truth. As Mark Twain once wrote: "It is my conviction that the Children's Theatre is one of the very great inventions of the twentieth century, and that its vast educational value will presently come to be realized. It's much the most effective teacher of morals and promoter of good conduct that the ingenuity of man has yet devised . . . its lessons are not taught wearily by book and dreary homily, but by visible and enthusing action; and they go straight to the heart, which is the rightest of right places for them. . . . " Occasionally a newspaper or magazine will provide a moving human interest story which will play beautifully.

Some years ago, I found in the *Reader's Digest* a dramatic, moving true story which I pounced upon at once. It not only concerned beautiful human relationships, but also contained all the requirements for improvisation, a beginning, a middle and a very satisfactory ending. The theme was used for a song which has become very popular, entitled, "Tie a Yellow Ribbon 'Round the Old Oak Tree." I was touched by the character of a released prisoner in the story who had heard nothing from his wife during his incarceration, even after he had written that he was to get an early parole, but he could not resist taking a bus toward his hometown. His conflict was great, however, for if he was no longer acceptable to his family he must not appear. Just before leaving prison, he wrote a final letter, asking his wife to give him a signal if she really wanted him home again. The "welcome home" sign was to be a bow of yellow ribbon tied to the old oak tree, near the bus station, a familiar rendezvous of their younger days. There was high drama in those last few minutes before the bus reached the little town. Only as it slowed down did he dare to face the window. His heart skipped a beat as he saw the old tree branches blossoming with yellow ribbons. He dashed to the door, his eyes full of tears, and gathered his smiling wife and children into his arms.

I shall explain how I prepared the above material for use by a teenage class in the hope that it will assist you, my readers, in adapting and revising a story for presentation to your class. First, realizing that my group was composed of girls only, one immediate decision was obvious; my released prisoner must be a woman. Next, I must find a reason for her imprisonment which would not dampen the sympathy of the other girl occupants of the bus. I decided that while her husband was out of work, she had allowed herself to get involved with some rather shrewd and shady characters in order to make a little extra money. Her motive was reasonable, and she was so naive she never bothered to investigate the appealing scheme which promised to pay her fifty percent on any piece of jewelry she sold in her neighborhood. It all seemed too good to be true. Not until she and several of her "bosses" had been arrested, did she realize that she was dealing in stolen goods. This part of the story I had to invent; any situation one presents must seem plausible to the young people involved. It would not have been enough just to say that the young woman had been paroled early; the background of the case is needed. Then we had to decide upon the scene itself. The story seemed to demand a bus interior. Then I asked myself some questions. Who would the other passengers be? How would they hear about the young woman's circumstances? Unless we could answer these questions, the audience would have no awareness of the real situation and there would be no drama, except that in the heart of the prisoner.

First, a title came: "Going Home" seemed right. Then, remembering the custom so popular recently for high school and college students to head for Florida during spring vacation, I decided that four of these girls could be passengers on the prisoner's bus, headed south. The little town in which the prisoner lived would be somewhere in Georgia. The girls had noticed the sad-eyed young woman who boarded the bus in Philadelphia, but in their excitement had paid her little attention. Finally, one of them realized that she sat near a window, looked out constantly and never left the bus at any of the food stops, nor had she spoken to anyone. This behavior aroused their curiosity. The scene would actually begin for us, I decided, when the girls boarded the bus after the third food stop, somewhere in the south. The curtain rises on the bus, empty except for the hunched, lonely figure still staring out the window. The four girls come in chattering and munching on sandwiches and popcorn. As they sit down behind the young woman, one calls attention to the fact that she must be starved, and again she had failed to leave the bus. They decide to offer her some popcorn and try to find out what is wrong; they are really concerned and would like to help if they can. Their offer is turned down, quietly, politely; she is not hungry. Not discouraged, they try to find out where she is going and they soon realize that she is trying to avoid direct answers. Then one girl ventures: "If there is something wrong and we could do something to help, we'd be glad to. It seems a shame for us to be happily off for a holiday while you sit here so miserable." Finally, after persistent questions, the young woman tells them her story about prison, her parole, the silence of her family during the whole time, her last-minute plea to her husband and the plan about the ribbons.

One girl suddenly sees the sign they are passing and reads the name of her little town which is only a few miles further. They all try to comfort the young woman, who can barely look up now. They assure her that the ribbon will be there as they eagerly watch from the bus windows. The prisoner, whose face is buried in her hands now, seems to be murmuring a fervent prayer. Eventually the bus slows down. The girl nearest the front shouts, "We're here. And there's the tree. LOOK! Look friend, quickly!" The young woman's quick glance is rewarded! There are hundreds of yellow ribbons and beneath the tree are two little boys and their smiling, eager father. The girls chatter almost incoherently in their joy! The young woman is too near tears to speak. The girls get her bag and practically push her off the bus.

Their noses are pressed against the glass as the bus starts to move. Then there are frantic waves and shouts of goodbye and perhaps words like these as the scene ends: "Those two darling little boys. She's holding both of them in her arms. And her husband's hugging all of them."

This incident, supposedly drawn from real life, has been used a dozen times with as many different groups of children. It has never failed to hold their interest, inspire sincere, believable dialogue, and touch hearts very deeply. The Christian lessons implied here are numerous — human sympathy, charity, forgiveness, unselfishness, sharing — all these are symbolic of sound Christian attitudes. The planning and playing of such a story is a more effective teacher than many sermons or church school lessons.

Although space will not allow the adaptation of other story material in this detailed manner, we can draw, from the treatment of this one, several important rules which should govern the preparation of any story.

1. Search diligently for incidents which will appeal to your age group and study them until you have thoroughly absorbed and digested every detail.

2. Decide what changes and/or additions you must make, what incidents can be used and which should be omitted.

3. Look at the characters carefully, keeping your own group in mind, and decide which ones are essential in your story and which can be deleted. You may even need some additional characters to complete your revised version.

4. Think through a possible setting. Where will the action take place? Try to include as much as possible in one scene. If you must make it a two- or three-scene story, then try to simplify the set changes.

5. Determine where, in the original story, your action will begin. You will remember that in "Going Home" discussed above, the scene opened effectively with the bus entirely empty, except for the lonely figure in the front seat. The sound of the laughter of the girls off stage offered a striking contrast.

6. Plan an effective ending which comes as soon as possible after the climax.

This homework done, the teacher will set down his new revised story, written in dialogue for the most part. He will leave no stone unturned in researching every detail of the background material of the story, the country, its customs and folklore. He will meet his group then, armed with a "new" manuscript and an abundant store of information related to the story, which he will use to enrich the discussion.

Some teachers will immediately wonder why reading the original story, as it appears, and helping the children to revise it for dramatization, is not recommended. My reason for not advocating this approach is based on several sad experiences which drove home an important lesson. Young children are not ready for group play writing, and they will surely feel a sense of failure and frustration if we permit them to attempt such a thing. They cannot be expected to visualize which incidents will best carry the plot forward or which characters to delete or add. Much time is wasted while one attempts to use everyone's ideas without seeming to reject even the most impractical. Some must be rejected, however, if part of the objective in the play-making project is to increase young people's feeling for the artistic form of drama. Their creative growth comes from the experience of improvising the dialogue and developing the characterizations. Skill in writing plays requires very special technical training; this is a challenge, which, in my opinion, is best reserved for another time. Perhaps an older group, wishing to devote a whole semester to oral play-making in an advanced English class, and eager to spend the time learning about dramatic structure, might successfully attempt this kind of task.

Crucial to the success of the project is the way in which the story is presented the first time. If the teacher is thoroughly familiar with his material, enthusiastic and dramatic in his presentation, an immediate affirmative response from the children will usually be his reward. If it is told, largely in dialogue form, instead of read, it will seem more alive and spontaneous. No one explains the importance of preparing and presenting the story dramatically better than Geraldine Siks. She says: ". . . to share a story creatively, a leader must first make the story her own . . . she reads it again for sheer enjoyment, edits and analyzes the moods and drama elements . . . she sees it happening, unfolding, in a series of vivid pictures . . . she identifies with the characters. . . . A story must become real and alive to a leader before he can make it live for others."

A lively group discussion should follow the first telling of the story. By posing skillful questions, the leader can emphasize the dramatic content and climax, clarify the relationship of the characters, and focus on the Christian aspects of the theme. He will explain the setting as he conceives it; interesting suggestions concerning the scene and the characters may come from the children. It is wise to accept as much as possible; if the ideas will not work dramatically, the wise teacher will make very clear his reasons for rejecting them. The next step is the retelling of the first *acting unit*. It is important to explain this term as it is used in this book. It refers to the dialogue between the first set of characters in the play; the unit ends when an entrance or exit made by one or more characters changes the nature of the conversation. This term, my own, does not refer to what one usually interprets as a scene, after which a curtain falls. Any dramatic story contains many more acting units than it does scenes. Although the story "Going Home" is a single scene which may play from five to eight minutes, it contains three *acting units.* The first unit concludes the conversation among the four girls as they board the bus, chattering about their vacation, and finally about the strange young woman who speaks to no one. The second acting unit includes the conversation of all five passengers, including the young ex-prisoner. When she is brought into the picture, the whole trend of the discussion changes. The climax of this unit comes when the bus stops at the little town beside the ribbon-bedecked tree. The third unit is really the denouement; it is the few moments after the prisoner leaves when the girls watch her greet her family and discuss what they see and how happy they are.

It is relatively simple for young people to improvise a conversation which centers about a single theme, but confusion abounds when several different subjects are attempted in unbroken sequence. Important ideas which move the plot are often forgotten and the results are unsatisfactory for everyone. If each unit is attempted separately, and the discussion centers only on the basic topic of dialogue in the unit, it is likely that all of the ideas presented in the preliminary talk will find their way into the conversation.

When the first acting unit is understood, the setting clear, and markers, such as chairs or stools, set up to suggest entrances, the teacher will ask for volunteers to play this section of the story. Usually many offers will come and interest will run high. If the unit requires three characters, the teacher might select three or four groups of three; she will ask which one will try the scene first. A lively group discussion should follow each playing. The students watching, especially those who are about to attempt the same scene, will have many suggestions. The teacher must always begin the discussion with an affirmative comment in order to set the mood for honest, constructive criticism. During these early improvisations, it is wise to refrain from interrupting with any suggestions or directions. The group is hopefully deep in picturing and imaginatively thinking in character; they should take the responsibility of continuing to the end of the unit.

On rare occasions when the dialogue seems to bog down completely, the scene must be stopped and started over again. This is usually an indication that the youngsters are attempting to improvise without really having become familiar with the story pattern. In such an instance, the teacher might say: "I am afraid we started to play the scene without being sure of what the conversation must include. Let's discuss it in greater detail, so we will all understand, shall we?" In this manner, he can supply the needed information for any of the inattentive young people, without really blaming anyone.

The second attempt by the same group will always improve. After the discussions and the playing by all three groups, the entire unit will probably have come to life; most of the important plot material will have been included and frequently some delightful original ideas will have enriched the scene.

In the same way, the second and third units may be attempted by several groups of children. By the end of the hour, the whole story will be familiar to everyone and the teacher will be ready to select several casts. His close observation will enable him to judge the imaginative power and flexibility of every member of the class. During the critique periods, following the first improvisations, the movement pattern — blocking is the theater term — and the balancing of the stage picture may be introduced. The following questions might be posed by the teacher after the first playing of the first unit of "Going Home." "Where do you think the girls should sit in the bus, in relationship to the prisoner? Wouldn't they want to talk about her quietly, without her noticing them?" "Yes, she might sit in the front seat, where she feels more isolated, and the girls could occupy several rows nearer the back. When they talk to her they might move forward to stand in the aisle or sit just behind her." This kind of discussion with the participants may elicit some valid new ideas and will help keep the interest of the whole group high. A healthy sense of total participation gives each individual a feeling of satisfaction, having shared in the final decisions.

If a program of short improvised plays is planned for a special occasion, when parents or other classmates become an audience, the teacher must be sure that everyone in his drama group is included. To play the same story twice, each time with a different cast, has often added interest to a program. Although the interpretations will be entirely different, each will be fresh, believable and honest. Whether four different stories are improvised for the "special occasion," or two stories are played by two different casts, the teacher is always responsible for the final selection of individuals for the roles. Casting done by young people invariably uncovers personal favoritism or hostility; embarrassing situations can result, seriously hurting the project. The teacher is the only one who, at this stage, knows the capabilities of his young people, the extent of their development, and their readiness to accept the responsibility for larger or smaller roles. He will undoubtedly already have won the confidence of his students. They will surely trust his judgment in casting with impartial wisdom and with the success of the whole project at heart.

When the time comes to select material for celebrating a specific occasion in the church school year, this often calls for something more ambitious than a few five-minute improvisations. Does the teacher automatically turn to the list of formal play scripts and forget his creative drama techniques entirely? That question can be answered affirmatively, but this is not, in most cases, advisable. It may be possible to find an appropriate story which naturally divides into four or five short episodes, each of which can be developed creatively. On the other hand, the best story may adapt well if some of the scenes are treated creatively, while most of the dialogue, which carries the plot, is assigned to older actors who are prepared to work creatively within the limits of a manuscript. Examples of both are given in chapter 7. The last play, based on St. Paul, is an example of the kind of material which naturally divides into a few short episodes to be developed creatively.

A scene from Dickens' A CHRISTMAS CAROL, produced by the Children's Theatre Association under the author's direction.

My own dramatization of Dickens' A CHRISTMAS CAROL is typical of the story which includes specific scenes. There is one in the old schoolroom, one in Fezziwig's warehouse, one at Fred's home (Scrooge's nephew), several at the Cratchits' house, a street scene, a prologue and an epilogue. Each of these lasts from five to ten minutes and is one of the visions experienced by Ebenezer Scrooge at the hands of the Spirits of Past, Present and Future, who visit him on Christmas Eve. This play was produced annually in Baltimore during the holiday season for sixteen years. The major characters, including Scrooge, Marley, Bob Cratchit, Fred, Master Fezziwig and the Spirits were all played by older teenagers or alumni from creative drama classes. The children and young people needed for each of the dream scenes were drawn from the current creative drama classes. The dialogue was recreated each season by the new group of young players, following the plot outline in our original manuscript. The result was a remarkably fresh, spontaneous, and believable presentation.

The following detailed explanation of the creative handling of such a scene within the formal play script may assist the teacher who decides to use this interesting and rewarding method. In the first section of the Dickens story, Scrooge is led by the Spirit of Christmas Past, in his dream, to his old schoolroom. Here he sees himself, a child of nine or ten, sitting with his fellow students just before the holiday recess. At the sound of the school bell, all the children except Scrooge jump up from their benches with delight at the prospect of the holiday. But poor little Ebenezer was doomed to spend a lonely fortnight in the empty school with its sour-faced Master. He was not wanted at home. The double cast of eight-to-ten-year-olds, when called together, listened to a dramatic telling of the story. The teacher pointed out the fact that there were three obvious subjects, implied by the plot, to give form to the first group conversation: 1) The joy of the anticipated holiday; 2) the children's sympathy for little Ebenezer's problem; 3) the arrival of the coach, with its new trappings, which was to take them off to the railroad station. Before the end of the second session together, each child and his counterpart (one never uses the term *understudy*) had decided upon his own dialogue contribution in each of the three subject areas.

To avoid confusion, each was given a number from one to six, thus establishing an order for speaking. As the school bell rang, the following dialogue might develop, concerning the long awaited holiday:

(1) Hooray! The holiday's here!

(2) At last . . . we're going home for Christmas!

(3) No more books for two whole weeks!

(4) I can hardly wait to see Granny. She's coming for Christmas.

(5) Mom says we're going to have a big goose.

(6) And plum pudding, too, I bet!

Once each child had decided upon the idea for his portion of the conversation, he retained it and repeated it at the next rehearsal. His counterpart used the same idea even though his phrasing might vary somewhat. In this way repetition was avoided.

Early in the rehearsals, the teacher suggested that at the sound of the bell, all of the children, except Ebenezer might rush to the little coat rack upstage on which a dozen nails held the scarfs and caps belonging to the students. This meant that their conversation about the holiday took place while they were preparing to leave. Then, as they turned back toward downstage, they would naturally see the lonely figure of Ebenezer sitting there on his bench, his head bowed. This sad sight provided motivation for the second topic of conversation. One child might say, "Poor Ebenezer; I'm sorry you can't go home for the holiday." As the others gathered around the little seated figure, each contributed something to this special topic. The spontaneity of this scene, as it began to take shape, and the genuine empathy it evoked from those watching it, were breathtaking!

Teachers observing this kind of demonstration are usually convinced that the application of the creative drama technique can be highly effective within the framework of the formal play. Mr. Dan Lipschutz, a visiting director of the Stockholm Children's Theatre, reported an interesting incident which occurred during his period of study at Northwestern University while he was directing *Mr. Popper's Penguins.* He wrote me: " . . . out of forty fifth- and sixth-grade children, I selected eighteen 'penguins'. Using improvisation at the auditions was most helpful. All of the penguin scenes, which should be most compelling for a young audience, were developed at rehearsals, creatively. I first motivated the action by establishing the dramatic conflict: Mr. Popper needed to raise money and the penguins desire to help him. Questions such as these brought interesting responses: 'What could birds do to make an exciting theater show? How could they entertain an audience?' 'Well,' said one, 'they could do acrobatics.' Another said, 'Maybe they could march because they always seem to walk in lines, anyway.' Dancing was a further suggestion. They had gathered these ideas from our trips to the zoo and from pictures. Through group discussion, we originated several scenes not included in the play version of the story. One of these scenes, incorporated in the final production, surpassed many of the others in vitality, freshness, and natural humor."

In developing a formal play creatively, most authorities feel that the leader assumes a role somewhat different from that played in the creative drama class. He must be especially adept at accepting and refining the children's suggestions, always remembering that his first responsibility is providing a fine theater experience for his young audience. The late Winifred Ward, a pioneer in the field of creative drama, was convinced that any play developed by children needs careful polishing and some direction if it is to be presented for an audience. It is certainly true that children derive much greater satisfaction from sharing their accomplishments, if they can be truly proud of what they have achieved. Obviously, the teacher must understand the fundamental dramatic elements of a good play, and basic principles of stage direction. Geraldine Siks' comment shows agreement: "If a creative dramatics leader is to help children create a play, she must know what makes a play . . . understand the fundamental drama elements that go into the making of a play."

6

Planning and Staging
The Longer Play

Whether one plans to present a half-hour (or longer) play for an audience, using creative drama techniques, or decides on the formal production of a scripted play to be memorized, a few organizational and directorial suggestions may help to avoid some pitfalls and give more life and vitality to the presentation. The ideas which follow are more or less applicable to both kinds of projects. In this section we will discuss the selection and preparation of material, the value of the play experience for both actors and audience, practical matters such as facilities, budgets, the cooperation of the other artists, musicians and costumers for example, planning and conducting rehearsals, and the qualifications of a successful director of a drama project for young people in the Church.

THE PLAY AND THE OCCASION

One of the keystones to success is the selection and preparation of interesting material appropriate for the occasion, the group performing, and the group watching. In the chapter devoted to more complex dialogue exercises, the basic tests for good material have already been mentioned. Since the same general rules apply to play selection, a "refresher" here may be in order.

(1) The content must be dramatic; the conflict should be clear; suggestions for exciting incidents which lead directly to a climax and a swift denouement are essential.

(2) The characters should be sharply defined, consistent, believable, real people.

(3) There should be a significant theme, dealing with worthwhile values and sound universal truths.

(4) The scenes should be few, and the staging requirements not too complex for implementing in the facilities available, whether it be the education building, a church hall, or the chancel.

(5) The story should be warm with human interest and appealing to the hearts and minds of both actors and audience.

PREPARATION AND PRESENTATION

Before presenting the story material to the group, the conscientious director will study it thoroughly. The purpose of this analytical look is to discover any extraneous incidents or characters, the deletion of which might strengthen the story line. Changing the order of events might also tighten the plot. He will always subject his revised material to the test question: Will this play satisfy the audience and actors for which it is planned? If an unequivocal affirmative reply is instantaneous, then he is ready to proceed. The director must feel confident that his participating young people will grow emotionally, spiritually and socially through this experience, and that their interest will be sustained through the weeks ahead. If the play comes alive with fresh, artistic, honest conviction, the empathy of the audience will be assured. The universal truths implicit in the dramatized human relationships will unconsciously become a strong influence on the life patterns of those on both sides of the footlights. These precious benefits will, of course, only accrue if the production is free of amateurish flaws, such as forgotten cues, late entrances, inappropriate costumes, lengthy and noisy scene shifts. Frances Durland makes an interesting distinction between the free creative dramatics exercises and the story-drama, as well as the difference in the director's responsibilities and objectives. She comments: "Immediately you will find yourself facing a different technique of procedure. There is considerable difference in the detail of rehearsal and objective . . . [formerly] your objectives were to set the group free by means of creative play. Now you are about to use that creative force to construct an art form."

THE COOPERATING ARTISTS

No matter how appealing a story or play may be, before deciding on its production, the wise director will consider carefully his facilities, the budget, the amount of qualified technical help he may expect and the cooperation of young people and their families in attending rehearsals promptly and regularly. All of these practical matters are vitally important. The most beautiful and moving story can be a ludicrous failure if technical help is missing at a critical time or facilities, promised for rehearsals, are denied. Even the inspired, imaginative director, who is working for a meaningful artistic whole, can fail to achieve his objective if there are no capable, cooperative

volunteers or professionals available. The setting, costumes, music, lighting, sound, and make-up are all vital contributing parts of a single unit. High technical production standards are absolutely essential, if the play presented in the church or the church school is to move the audience with its message. This does not imply the need for an extravagant budget; it does mean that theater is an art and it is better entirely omitted from the program than desecrated by shabby, inappropriate staging. The audio-visual elements, to which we have just referred, are almost as important as the script and acting ability of the cast. One must always give children in the audience credit for discriminating taste and keen powers of observation. They notice, often more readily than adults, a tasteless costume or an incompatible set piece. Although settings, costumes and lighting effects may be simple, they must be in keeping with the theme and period of the play or they will seriously detract from its impact.

Should scene changes be necessary, a skillful, unobtrusive plan must be evolved so that the mood of the audience is not disturbed. A darkened acting area or the use of background music may help to bridge this transitional moment. Such music should, if possible, originate with a creative musician. One is sometimes fortunate enough to find a talented, flexible church organist who will study the script and offer suggestions for the use of background music to deepen certain moments in the play. If, in addition, he will compose and play this original music, one is especially blessed. For many years I was one of those favored few, thanks to my good friend, Virginia Reinecke, a brilliant concert pianist and a composer. As Miss Reinecke read lines or heard them spoken, she seemed to hear their meaning in music. Such support for pantomimic action, long stage crosses, subtly deepening or fore-shadowing a mood, is invaluable. If such talent is not available, then perhaps another member of the parish, who is musically inclined, will become interested and assist in the play project.

The same applies to the costumer, the stage designer, and the light technician. If there are no such talents to be found willing to assist on a volunteer basis, then the director must turn to other sources in the community, or as a last resort, engage professional help. These suggestions are not intended to discourage or intimidate the would-be director; they are meant as a practical warning which, if heeded, can prevent many heartaches and disappointments.

REHEARSALS

Every individual involved with the play project — designers, musicians, technicians, actors — should be given a mimeographed sheet designating rehearsal times and places, performance dates and any other information necessary to a smooth-running project. The director will have studied all of this material and made his decisions well in advance, being careful to allow plenty of time for work on each unit of the play. The division of a long play into workable rehearsal units (sections in which the same characters appear) is absolutely essential. A unit of four or five typewritten pages may need only five rehearsals; one twice the length may require eight to ten meetings. Only the members of the cast appearing in a specific unit are asked to rehearse together at any given time. This procedure will hold the interest of all those present, for the material is of serious moment to them all. No one is wasting time; everyone is actively concerned. Young people who are kept waiting, doing nothing, become restless

and often troublesome. The *unit rehearsal* system eliminates this kind of problem.

Another advantage of a carefully planned, typed or printed rehearsal schedule is the clout it carries, as it unmistakably announces the director's seriousness of purpose. Such a schedule provides each participant with a panoramic view of the next month's activities. Individual calendars can be marked and the necessary dates cleared for rehearsals and performances. The psychological effect is an affirmative one; the project assumes an aura of importance and dignity. Attendance at rehearsals, requested formally in writing, will be very impressive. Should illness or unavoidable circumstances prevent attendance, the participant can notify the director promptly, because the latter's address and telephone number are included on the rehearsal sheet. It has been my experience that a month to five weeks is ample time for the preparation of an hour-long play, if several rehearsals of the longer units can be scheduled every week. Anticipation and interest in any project is dulled when its completion takes two or three months and the spontaneity and freshness seem to disappear.

The creative director will handle the first few rehearsals with great care. His cast will already be familiar with the characters and story of the play. This first acquaintance will have been made during the improvisations usually planned in connection with the casting. At the first rehearsal of each unit, however, it will be necessary to refresh memories on the content of this special section. A quick synopsis may be given by the director or by one of the cast who may eagerly volunteer. The next procedure is the reading through of the unit from the written manuscripts prepared for those taking the major roles. The younger children, who will work creatively for the most part, will listen, and the director will fill in their thoughts, using his own manuscript. A general discussion may follow this first run-through of the unit. If the director will pose some significant questions, he can soon discover whether everyone in the group understands the character relationships and the plot development. If time permits, a second reading may be helpful. This time, the younger ones will probably offer to fill in their own thoughts; these may only slightly resemble the original written dialogue but often they will contribute fresh, exciting ideas which will be very appropriate.

At this point the director should explain the visual aspects of the scene as he has conceived it. A rough sketch will help to clarify the verbal picture. Entrances and exits will be noted and questions and suggestions from the group should be encouraged. When agreement has been reached, a few chairs or stools are placed to mark off limitations of space, walls, furniture, and exits. The general movement pattern of the major characters may be suggested by the director and important entrances described. Just enough information is provided to facilitate the next procedure — a walk-through of the first section of the unit being rehearsed, using one of the two casts. By this time the flow of both action and dialogue should be fairly smooth.

An evaluation and analysis should follow this first attempt; both the casts and the director should participate in the discussion. Some suggestions for movement or dialogue changes may be forthcoming. The director will incorporate the suggestions he considers useful in his overall plan and reject those which he feels are inappropriate. He will always be careful to give valid reasons for such rejection, thereby helping his young people to deepen their understanding of artistic dramatic form.

The second cast will now walk through the same scene; usually this second attempt is even smoother and more convincing. The major characters will probably make little use of their manuscripts, even though they still carry them. Young people who have been working creatively for some time, are eager to free themselves of the uncomfortable restraint imposed by the typewritten sheets in their hands.

Each rehearsal unit will be handled in the manner just described. After several weeks the little play will begin to come to life. Each child will have shared in its creation, even though the basic manuscript has been prepared by the director in order to make sure of the dramatic form, and the consistent forward movement of the plot line. As the time for the performance draws near, it is safe to offer a few technical suggestions to the young players. Unsuitable words or slang expressions which may have crept into the dialogue should be eliminated at this point. The pace of an important scene may need quickening, or some climactic moment pointed up by effective changes in timing. At this stage of the project, the young people will have completely identified with the characters they are playing; their interpretation will remain fresh and believable despite some directorial advice. At least three final rehearsals should be held on the stage, or in the specific area selected for the performance. On these occasions, the entire story will be played through twice; the entire double cast will be present. Costumes, properties, stage settings, and make-up will all be used. The lighting planned for the performance will be ready for these last sessions, as will the music and/or sound effects. The volunteer committees in charge of these technical matters will have been reminded of the deadlines well in advance, so that they will be ready to accept their responsibility for their part of the project during the final rehearsals and performances.

Even when all the *acting units* of the little play are finally welded together, supplemented by all the artistic and technical "accessories," some minor catastrophes may still occur despite careful planning. A soldier's spear may have been forgotten, the King's tunic may be a perfect fit on king number one but be far too small for king number two. The wise director will accept the problems and use his ingenuity in solving them creatively for the moment. It is his responsibility at this crucial moment to keep all spirits high and all hearts relaxed and happy! Although we are striving to give to the audience a moving and aesthetically sound experience in good theater, we must never forget that we are also indebted to the young participants. During these weeks of working and sharing together, each youngster's sense of identity should have grown considerably. As he has acquired new skills in communicating thought and feeling, he should have developed more self-confidence. From his own new sense of achievement and the attitude of his peers toward him, he naturally builds his self-esteem. Every teacher-director will consciously strive to foster this kind of growth, knowing that it is a far more valid objective than an unflawed stage production. Hopefully, both goals can be achieved simultaneously.

THE TEACHER-DIRECTOR

Although most of the essential attributes of the successful teacher-director have been discussed in Chapter 3 as requirements for the creative drama leader, a few additional suggestions, appropriate largely to the director of Church-related groups, may be useful. Especially in our complex and confused society, young people, in their efforts to develop a sense of direction and self-esteem, need some worthwhile models with whom to identify. Reuel Howe speaks eloquently on this point: "He [the child] needs the association with men and women who are capable of and practice a reasonable, wholesome relationship with each other . . . who have convictions, who can distinguish between right and wrong. He needs counselors who can help him bring together and concentrate his various and fluctuating drives and interests, and who are not dismayed by the inconsistencies that may accompany his development. Finally he needs help in acquiring a sense of vocation, of being called to something that is greater than himself, which will draw him forth as a participant in the deepest meaning of life."

The director does, of course, need training in the art of drama and related fields, but he has a far greater need as he begins to work with his young people's group on the Easter or Christmas presentation. He must recognize and accept his exciting and challenging opportunity to deepen their faith and understanding of Christian living. The religion of the leader who can accomplish this must, "instead of being a defense against life, provide courage to move into life and become a part of it . . . [his] reverence for God is not confined to the sanctuary but is exhibited in responsible relations with people."

Dr. Frank Whiting, former chairman of the Theatre Arts Department of the University of Minnesota, an experienced children's theater director, also offers wise advice which should prove helpful to the director of the Church-affiliated play for young people. He believes that any teacher-director must understand that this life is essentially a life of service, that there is little room for egocentricity and pride. He should be prepared to work long hours for the pure joy of it. He must have a great appreciation for and familiarity with dramatic literature and an even more sensitive understanding of children's literature and child psychology. Although Dr. Whiting believes that young people's theater should assume a position of prestige in today's world, he feels that this can only happen if enough directors can be found who are ready to dedicate their love of theater and their love of children to the cause. Let us hope that there are many who will strive to become worthy of this assignment!

Because there are a number of volumes which contain technical guidelines for directing, setting, lighting and costuming a play, detailed discussion on these points has been omitted here. A good list of reference books covering such subjects appears in the appendix. For directors desirous of understanding my own approach to this subject, I recommend a careful study of Chapters 10 and 11 of my text, *Creative Play Acting*, published by the Ronald Press Company of New York.

7

The Play's
The Thing

In this section, we have gathered some manuscript plays — short
ones, long ones — all of which have been created by the author with
working groups of children and young people. Most often they have
been prepared for presentation on a special occasion in the Church
Year, a young people's fellowship meeting, a school or a youth
workshop. This is their first appearance in print. A short resume
precedes each play; this is done in order to facilitate the leader's
selection of material to meet his specific needs. Suggestions for staging
are also included. The short plays may be produced by obtaining
written permission from the author.

Since you, the reader, may be providing a "premiere" for one or
more of the plays, the author invites, no, *encourages* you to send her
your reaction and that of your players and your audience. She also
takes pleasure in urging you and your group to feel free to improvise
on the manuscript provided. It will be best used when it can serve as a
basic sketch to be polished and refined by your children's creative
imaginations.

A LITTLE GIRL'S PRAYER

A dramatization based on the story of the baby Moses and the
discovery of his hiding place.

Characters

RUTH, Moses' mother
MIRIAM, Moses' sister
JONATHAN, Moses' brother
1ST EGYPTIAN BOY

2ND EGYPTIAN BOY
AZNATH, Pharaoh's daughter
FERON, Aznath's brother
CLARON, Feron's handmaid

Scene

The scene is a secluded spot near a river which runs close to the
Egyptian Pharaoh's palace. As the curtain rises, Ruth, Moses' mother,
comes on from stage left carrying the basket cradle she has made to
hide her baby from the Pharaoh's men. The Egyptian ruler, fearful of
the rumor that a Jewish child may become a threat to his power, has
ordered all Hebrew baby boys to be put to death. Ruth looks about
fearfully; when she is sure that she is alone, she carefully places the

basket among some tall grasses at the edge of the river, hurries off left, and returns at once with her precious baby.

RUTH: My poor little one! How glad I am that you cannot know the sadness that is in my heart. Ah! You are smiling! That's right, my son. Be happy and rest well in your strange new cradle. (She puts him gently in the basket.) God will protect you and send the gentle breeze to rock you to sleep.

MIRIAM: (*enters from left and is startled*) Mother! What are you doing to my baby brother? Why are you putting Moses in the river?

JONATHAN: (*who accompanies her*) Yes, Mother, why?

RUTH: (*alarmed*) Sh! Be still children. Someone may hear you! Be still!

JONATHAN: But mother, the water is so cold! He will not be as safe here as he is in his bed at home. Why must he sleep here?

RUTH: Because we must hide him away, Jonathan.

MIRIAM: But why, mother?

RUTH: Because hard times have come to our people here in Egypt now that the new Pharaoh rules. You see, he is afraid that the Hebrews will become stronger than his own people, so he has ordered that every baby Hebrew boy be killed.

JONATHAN: But it's wicked to kill little children; God will surely punish him.

RUTH: Yes, God will surely punish him one day.

MIRIAM: (*tearfully*) But I don't want our baby brother to go away! He has been with us for such a little while.

JONATHAN: And he's so good, and wise; he already seems to understand everything I say to him.

RUTH: Yes, he is very wise. I often think as I watch his face that God must have planned important things for him to do when he sent him to earth. That is why I have made a basket, with a cover, so that we may hide him away here in the tall grass during the day and only take him home late at night, when he will be safe with us. Come, Jonathan, help me to fasten the cover now, and then we must all go to work with father in the field.

MIRIAM: Oh dear, I hate to leave him here alone!

RUTH: Then perhaps you could stay for a little while, Miriam, and sing to him so that he will go to sleep and watch to see that he is not disturbed.

MIRIAM: Oh yes, mother, I should like to do that. Please do let me stay.

RUTH: Very well, child. But be sure to keep well hidden should anyone pass by.

MIRIAM: Yes, mother, I will.

JONATHAN: (*as he leans over cradle*) Goodbye little brother, rest well until we return.

RUTH: (*at cradle*) Farewell little Moses. God will protect you. Take care, Miriam!

MIRIAM: Yes, mother. (*Ruth and Jonathan exit at left. Miriam looks carefully in every direction and then kneels near the basket.*) Dear Heavenly Father, please don't forget to watch over our baby. He's just a little thing, but I know he will grow to love you and serve you as we do, if you will just let him live. (*She stops suddenly, and listens as if God has answered, telling her not to be afraid.*) Thank you, God. I won't be afraid any more! (*She speaks quietly to the baby.*) Be happy little brother, for you are sailing in a tiny boat and the wind is rocking you to sleep. (*As she finishes, she hears boys' voices off right; she runs up left to hide in the tall grass.*)

1ST BOY: (*off*) Let's go and get some of the branches down by the river's edge.

2ND BOY: All right. (*They come on stage.*) Look, there are some tall ones. (*They approach the spot where Miriam is hiding.*) Mother will like these. They'll be good enough to decorate for the feast even if the Pharaoh himself should come to dine with us.

1ST BOY: (*who is closer to the river*) Look, Tarik. What's that?

2ND BOY: (*casually looking over his shoulder*) Oh, it's just an old basket — probably belongs to one of those Hebrew slaves. Just like them to leave their things lying about.

1ST BOY: (*approaching basket*) Let's get it before it breaks loose and floats down stream.

2ND BOY: Oh no — why bother? Let it go! It will serve the careless woman right to lose her basket. She should take better care of her belongings. Come on! It's getting late! (*He picks up the branches he has gathered.*) We'd better take these home or mother will think we haven't found any.

1ST BOY: All right. But I sure would like to take the basket with us. We might be missing something, Tarik. There might be treasure hidden in it.

2ND BOY: What? Whoever heard of a Hebrew with treasure? That's a joke! You forget, Nieman, the Hebrews are the Pharaoh's slaves. (*They go off right talking and Miriam crawls out of her hiding place and crosses to look into the basket.*)

MIRIAM: Oh, that was a narrow escape, baby brother. And you were a good little fellow not to cry out at those Egyptian boys, for if you had they would have taken you to the Pharaoh's guards! (*Aznath, her handmaiden, and her brother Feron are heard talking off right.*)

AZNATH: (*off*) Come, let us rest here for a moment beside the river before we return to the palace. (*Miriam runs to hide again.*)

FERON: But we'll be late for the Lord's feast, sister, unless we hurry back. Besides, I don't see what's so beautiful about the river bank.

AZNATH: But it's so quiet and peaceful here, and the wind sings such a lovely tune in the tall grass. Listen, Feron!

HANDMAID: (*who has discovered the basket*) Mistress . . . look! Look at this little basket floating by the bank. (*The other two approach the bank. Miriam is deeply troubled.*)

AZNATH: Why, it's made of grass all covered with tar to keep the water out. It's like a little boat. This must be the work of some Hebrew woman; it's so finely done.

FERON: You'd better not let father hear you talk so of Hebrew women. The Pharaoh's daughter has no right to say such things! You know he's trying to get rid of those people as fast as he can.

AZNATH: Well, I don't agree with father, and I think he's being very cruel to them. Bring me the basket, Claron. Let's see whether it is as well made inside as out. (*She sits on an old log near the bank, at right of center. Feron sits at her right.*)

HANDMAID: Yes, my lady. (*She gets the basket and puts it down beside Aznath.*)

AZNATH: (*lifting the cover*) Look, Claron . . . look! It's a baby, a smiling baby boy!

FERON: A Hebrew boy! Good! Father will reward you for this, Aznath. Maybe he'll give me something, too. This is one his guards won't have to search for. Here, let me take him, I'll get rid of him myself!

MIRIAM: (*who can stand this no longer, comes out of her hiding place and throws herself at Aznath's feet*) Oh please, my lady, please have mercy on my little brother. Please I beg you!

AZNATH: (*gently lifting her up*) Who are you, child?

MIRIAM: My name is Miriam, and I am a Hebrew. I was set here to watch my brother and I couldn't bear it if any harm should come to him!

FERON: (*delighted*) I told you! It is a Hebrew boy! Let me have him, Aznath!

AZNATH: (*holding the baby in her arms*) No, Feron. Take your hands off, at once. Have no fear, Miriam. I like the little fellow. I promise you he is quite safe with me. I should dearly love to have him for my own, to care for him and bring him up in the palace as though he were my own son.

MIRIAM: Oh, thank you, my lady. You are so good. But . . . but . . . we will miss him so . . . if . . .

AZNATH: I know, of course, you will miss him. But you know the Pharaoh's decree. And I promise he will be safe with me.

CLARON: But Mistress, a Hebrew child! What will the Pharaoh say?

FERON: (*scoffing*) That's what I'd like to know.

AZNATH: He will say nothing, Feron. Father's first wish is for my happiness. I know this little boy will comfort my lonely hours and bring me joy. Some day, perhaps he will be a great man, of whom we will be proud.

FERON: A Hebrew? A great man? Nonsense! (*In disgust he walks off at right.*)

AZNATH: Miriam, child, could you possibly find me a good nurse for the child and bring her to the palace?

MIRIAM: (*suddenly thinking of her mother*) Oh yes, my lady. I know the very best nurse in all the land. She is a Hebrew woman, the wife of Levi.

AZNATH: Very well, then. You bring her to the Palace garden tomorrow morning. Claron will meet her at the North gate. I will have my steward give her proper robes and show her to her quarters. (*She starts off with the baby, then turns.*) You're a good child, Miriam, and you may come whenever you like to see your little brother.

MIRIAM: Oh, thank you, my lady, thank you. (*Aznath and Claron exit at right.*) Think of it! My mother will go to the palace and my baby brother will be spared! (*She falls on her knees.*) I was afraid, a little bit afraid, dear God, but only for a minute. And I'll never be again, I promise. I'll always trust you now, always. Thank you, dear God, for answering my prayer.

CURTAIN

THE KINDLY STAR

This little play was prepared for a children's service in the chapel of The Church of the Redeemer, Baltimore, Maryland. It was successfully presented several times, in the chancel, the pulpit and the center aisle. Instead of a curtain, several large screens, moved by adults, covered the change from the scene in the hills to the manger scene. The use of a children's choir and the church organist added much to the production. It can be presented on any stage, in the educational building, or church hall. If a stage curtain is available, the use of the screens can be eliminated. In this case a small platform (instead of the pulpit) must be placed below the curtain line, downstage right; chairs should be placed so that the center aisle will be available for the procession. Simple but appropriate controlled lighting is important.

Characters

THOMAS, a shepherd
NATHAN, another shepherd
SIMON, another shepherd
DAVID, a young shepherd boy
ANGEL's voice (angel need not appear)

THE THREE KINGS
MARY, Jesus' Mother
JOSEPH, her Husband
THE KINDLY STAR of Bethlehem

Scene 1

In the hills, overlooking the city of Bethlehem on the Holy Night. Two shepherds and a shepherd boy are resting near a small fire against some protecting rocks at left of center. Their flocks are roaming nearby. Simon and the boy David sit on the ground, David is holding a tiny lamb. Thomas is gathering some more wood for the fire at right.

THOMAS: (*moving toward the fire with an armful of small branches*) It's cold tonight, friends, and the wind is strong. Too bitter to get any rest, I fear.

SIMON: Aye, Thomas, it is! It's a hard life a shepherd leads, tending his sheep day and night. There is never time for rest.

THOMAS: What hour is it, Simon? It must be nearly dawn by now.

SIMON: I think not, Thomas. No sign of light in the sky, and Nathan has not yet returned from Bethlehem with our supplies.

DAVID: (*stretching*) I hope he comes soon. I'm hungry!

THOMAS: (*kindly*) I know, Lad. You are young to begin to live the shepherd's life. It *is* hard for you.

DAVID: Oh, no, Thomas. I love tending the sheep, especially the new lambs like this one. He's so soft and warm, and he likes it when I hold him in my arms like this. (*He cuddles the little lamb in his arms.*)

SIMON: Well, you'll make a fine shepherd one day because you're learning early that your first duty is to watch over your flock, winter and summer.

DAVID: Yes, I am, Simon. I already know that the sheep must never be left alone — never!

THOMAS: It's not always easy to remember that. Tonight, for instance, I am sure we should all have liked to go to Bethlehem with Nathan.

SIMON: Yes, indeed. The place must be alive with travellers come to pay their taxes. It's a sight I did not want to miss. Just look there . . . at the town. (*He moves toward down right to look off.*) Lights are twinkling everywhere, and usually, at this hour, darkness covers the sleeping city.

DAVID: And you stayed here with the sheep, you and Thomas.

THOMAS: Yes, we did, boy! Because we're shepherds, we stayed!

SIMON: Well, you two better try to get a little rest while the fire still burns. I think it's my turn to watch. I'll stand here by the path to Bethlehem where I can see the sheepfold and still watch for Nathan's return. (*He stands to right of center, and the others move closer to the fire, wrap their robes about them and seem to fall asleep.*)

THOMAS: The rest will be welcome, Simon.

DAVID: Yes, it will, for me and my lamb, too!

(*A hymn may be sung here if desired. "O Little Town of Bethlehem" is appropriate. After one or two verses, Nathan comes hurriedly onstage from off right. He is carrying their bread and cheese and some wine.*)

NATHAN: At last, Thomas, at last, I have brought your supper. It is a miracle that I got back to you before dawn.

SIMON: What happened, Nathan? Your eyes are shining with excitement!

NATHAN: I *am* excited, and with good reason. Let's wake the others; I want you all to hear the news.

SIMON: Yes . . . I'll stir them. Thomas, David . . . (*He shakes them gently*) wake up . . . wake up, Nathan has returned from Bethlehem with news for us.

DAVID: (*getting up, sleepily*) Did he bring our supper, too? That's what I want to know.

NATHAN: (*laughing*) Yes, Lad. You'll have your bread and cheese. (*Opens his pouch.*) Here you are. Now, sit down and eat, all of you.

(*The others murmur their thanks, take their portions of food and sit by the fire. Nathan remains standing.*)

SIMON: Now, what is this exciting message, Nathan?

THOMAS: Yes, make haste and tell us.

NATHAN: Well, as I left the inn, I was making my way with difficulty through the crowded streets toward our old path to these hills. The market place was humming with people as if it were mid-day. Whole families gathered about little fires, huddling together to keep warm. Men were drinking and singing and telling tales; travellers they were, from all over Palestine, come to pay their taxes. Apparently, every inn and private dwelling-place was full. Some say there's not a bed to be had in Bethlehem tonight for any price. Finally, when I saw my way was completely blocked, I decided on the longer path, the one that meets the main road from the east. I had just left the outskirts of the town when I heard the sound of camels' hoofs, and then, quite suddenly, I came face to face with a rich caravan from the east — Persia, I believe it was.

DAVID: Where is Persia, cousin? I never heard of it.

SIMON: Hundreds of miles to the east of us, lad. Now go on, Nathan. What happened then?

NATHAN: A gentleman dismounted, dressed like a King he was. He bowed very low and asked if I knew where the King of the World was to be born this night.

THOMAS: King of the World? What did he mean?

NATHAN: He said that he and his two friends, two other eastern Kings, had learned from their ancient prophets that, on this night, in the country of Judea, would be born a child who would become the saviour of the world.

SIMON: Could he mean the Messiah whom our Prophets promised us?

NATHAN: I don't know. I only know that they were told that they would be given a sign — a great light in the Heavens that would move before them and stop over the place where the baby lay.

THOMAS: And the sign, Nathan, have they seen it yet?

NATHAN: No. They watch and wait for it on the road below; their eyes are fixed on the Heavens. They are sure that it will come before long; and, somehow, I feel that they speak the truth. . . . There is something in the air . . . tonight. . . . (*All are silent for a moment and then a strange glow begins to appear in the sky. The choir hums or sings softly the Gloria. As it fades, the Angel's voice is heard through the music; the shepherds fall on their knees.*)

ANGEL: Fear not, friends, for behold I bring you glad tidings of great joy which shall be to you and to all people. For unto you is born this day, in the City of David, a Saviour, which is Christ the Lord. And this shall be a sign unto you. Ye shall find the babe wrapped in swaddling clothes and lying in a manger. (*Again the choir sings, building to a climax and then the music gradually fades and the glow in the sky disappears.*)

NATHAN: (*rising from his knees*) Did you hear? Did you? It is just as the King said! The voice of the Angel said it, too. It is the Saviour of the World!

DAVID: (*standing and looking down right suddenly sees a light in the heavens*) Look, Nathan, Thomas, look! It is the sign — the moving star!

SIMON: It is. It's a star that was not there before. (*The star light increases.*)

THOMAS: It grows brighter now, see!

NATHAN: And it is moving. Slowly but surely, it moves toward Bethlehem! (*All eyes follow the star.*)

DAVID: Oh, please Nathan, can't we go with the Kings? Can't we go to worship the new baby Saviour? Please — the star is calling us to come!

NATHAN: Yes, David is right. We must go, friends, and each one of us will take a gift to offer to our blessed King.

THOMAS: I have a few gold coins in my pouch.

SIMON: And I have a bag of rare herbs I have been collecting.

THOMAS: (*suddenly*) Wait, my friends — we're forgetting — we're forgetting that we are shepherds. We cannot leave our sheep in an open field on the hillside on a night like this!

DAVID: That's right, Thomas. One of us must stay!

SIMON: Let us draw lots, then, for it will be a hardship for the one who must remain on watch.

DAVID: (*after thinking seriously for a moment*) No, please, Simon. Don't draw lots. I am the youngest; let me stay and take care of the sheep. (*The others are astonished.*)

THOMAS: But David, that seems hardly fair. It was you who saw the star first of all.

DAVID: I know Thomas, but it's best for you to go. Make haste, you three, while the star is there to lead you.

NATHAN: The boy is good, and perhaps he is right, friends. It would be a long, cold trip for him. He would be better here! Come, let us be on our way! (*He starts off at right.*)

SIMON: Thank you, David. And do keep the fire going, to keep yourself warm.

DAVID: Yes, Simon, I will!

THOMAS: And don't worry, David. We'll be back soon after daybreak.

DAVID: May God bless your journey! (*Thomas and Simon go off right, following Nathan. David waves as he watches them disappear. He then returns, wraps himself with his robe and lies down near the fire, soon falling asleep. Suddenly the strength of the star's light seems to waken him. He looks up into the brightness.*) Dear, kindly Star, shine brightly and lead them to the King. . . . (*He starts to lie down but then decides to speak again*) Little star, I'd like to make a wish even though I know it can't come true. I wish — I wish that I, too, could see the Saviour of the World tonight. (*He lies down again, and rests. The choir sings or hums "Silent Night." As the music fades, the Star softly rises in the pulpit or platform down right. A light picks up her face.*)

STAR: David — David! Did I hear you speak to me?

DAVID: (*stirring, wakens slowly*) Did someone call my name? (*He looks about, sees the Star and is amazed*) Oh . . . who . . . who. . . .

STAR: I am the Star, David, the Star of Bethlehem. I have been leading your shepherd friends and the Kings from the east to the manger where the baby Jesus lies.

DAVID: The baby Jesus, is that the King's name? (*Star nods assent*) And he is lying in a manger? (*David sounds shocked and incredulous. He walks down stage into the nave so that curtains may close to facilitate changing to the manger scene.*)

STAR: Yes, David, because there was no room at the inn.

DAVID: They have found him then, the King of the World?

STAR: Yes, I can see them from here. They are coming to worship him, now.

DAVID: Oh, please, kindly Star, could you — could you somehow let me see it, too? I wanted to go with them but — but —

STAR: I know, David. You offered to stay and watch the sheep instead. That was fine of you, boy! That's why I came when you called.

DAVID: You mean, you mean you *will* show me?

STAR: Yes, David. If you'll come up here with me, I can let you see, through my eyes, all that is happening in Bethlehem.

DAVID: (*still incredulous, goes up into the pulpit with the Star still carrying his little lamb.*) Oh, thank you, dear Star. Thank you! It's what I wanted more than anything! (*Organ music starts as the curtain opens on the Manger scene with only Mary and Joseph. The shepherds come up the aisle and kneel.*) There they are! There are Thomas and Nathan and Simon! (*Choir begins the hymn, "We Three Kings of Orient Are" as the Kings come up the aisle and offer their gifts. As the last King bows and takes his position, David speaks.*)

DAVID: Look, dear Star. Everyone is taking a gift to the baby Jesus. I have nothing but my newest lamb. Do you think that I could take that?

STAR: Yes, David. Take it to him. He'll like that best of all. (*David goes down to center of nave and approaches the manger, offers his lamb to Joseph, and kneels. The little Star disappears as the spotlight fades. The choir sings an appropriate hymn. Gradually lights fade out on the manger scene.*)

CURTAIN

"PRIDE COMETH . . ."

The ideas for this play come directly from Bible sources. One can see, by referring to the original story, how certain parts of the material have been rearranged and enlarged upon in order to make the script come to life. Any incident, dramatic in content, can be so prepared for use in creative dramatizations. While plot is the fundamental, indispensable feature of a drama, character is often more interesting; its change and growth is more significant. The plot shows us what happens to the protagonist, or chief personage. On his character depend his responses to these happenings. The story of Naaman sketches the picture of a powerful general who is consumed with pride over his own military successes. He is finally forced to listen to the suggestion of a poor Jewish slave girl, the very child whom Naaman's soldiers had dragged away from her home. The story centers around the confrontation of this proud general, without spiritual resources, and Elisha, the prophet, a man of vision, unmoved by the offer of priceless treasures, anxious only to serve his God. Naaman's glory suddenly crumbles when he discovers his leprosy; neither the priests of Rimmon nor his King Ben Hadad can help him. It is then that the little slave girl begs her master to go to the prophet Elisha, for she knows that her God has great healing powers. Naaman is shocked that Elisha will accept no gifts, nothing to sacrifice to his God; he is equally shocked when he is asked only to bathe in the River Jordan. In revising this story for dramatization, we must ask ourselves several questions: 1) Why should the little maid feel so kindly toward Naaman, if she was snatched from her home by his soldiers? 2) What sort of man was Naaman? 3) What effect did leprosy have upon his career, his friendships, his character? 4) What are the motives behind his actions? 5) Are additional characters needed to throw the proper light upon our main characters?

Characters

NAAMAN
ZARA, Naaman's wife
NAAMAN'S MOTHER

HADASSAH, the slave girl
ELISHA, the Hebrew Prophet
GOHAZI, Elisha's servant

NAAMAN'S SERVANT

Scene 1

The royal apartments in the beautiful home of Naaman, the general of the Syrian armies. There is a divan at stage left, a regal chair at right, before which stands a low table. A small bench stands against the upstage wall. Rich colors and fabrics used in the decor suggest the wealth and prestigious position of the home's owners. At rise Zara is seated at right, near the table, sorting beautiful jewels. Naaman's mother reclines on the divan at left; Hadassah brings in a brass tray with coffee from left offering it first to the elderly lady on the divan.

HADASSAH: Your coffee, Madame.

MOTHER: Nay child, take it to your Mistress and bring me the sweetmeats.

HADASSAH: Yes, Madame. (*Hadassah crosses to the table at right, places the coffee cup on the table and takes the brass bowl of dates from table to the older woman at left.*)

ZARA: My Lord's bravery has indeed filled his palace with silver and gold, Mother. He has generously showered me with silk and embroidery and jewels. (*Hadassah has put tray on bench upstage.*)

MOTHER: True, Zara, but I am troubled about Naaman today. He was very quiet this morning; he seemed anxious about something. Can it be that the King's favor is turning to someone else?

ZARA: (*rising and crossing toward divan at left*) Nay, mother. That is not possible. Surely you know that he is the favorite at the King's court. Why only yesterday he summoned my Lord to his presence and gave him a bronze necklace with a ruby in the center as big . . . yes . . . as big as Hadassah's eye. It's said to be a magical jewel that has power over all evil spirits. Now no enemy arrow can touch him. (*Hadassah has moved to table down left, to arrange it and take coffee cup back to tray.*)

MOTHER: Perhaps Naaman is planning some new attack . . . to lead an army against Bashan or Israel. . . .

ZARA: Nay, mother, that cannot be. (*She crosses to her chaise*) Naaman has already brought deliverance to Syria; he has subdued almost all their enemies!

HADASSAH: (*who has seen Naaman approaching from left, runs to center*) Mistress, lily of the morning, behold my Lord comes. You can see him, yonder. (*She gestures toward the left.*)

ZARA: So he is. Quickly, my veil, Hadassah, and my pearls. (*Hadassah fetches these from bench upstage and comes down to right to arrange them for her mistress.*)

MOTHER: The dear child always has such a glad welcome for my son!

ZARA: Yes, she remembers thankfully how Naaman saved her from that rough soldier. Don't you child?

HADASSAH: Oh yes! He was beating me to death, Princess, because I could not carry his heavy bundle. I was so tired. I just couldn't!

And my Lord paid him gold to release me and then he brought me here to serve you. I was so grateful! (*Naaman enters at down left. Hadassah retreats to up center and Zara sits in her chair at right.*)

MOTHER: (*as Naaman bows low over her hand*) Peace to my Lord. Is all well with you, my son?

ZARA: The blessings of Rimmon crown my Lord who is the light of mine eyes! (*She rises, bows, and starts toward him at right of center with arms outstretched. He motions her to stand back.*)

NAAMAN: Nay, Zara, come not a step closer! Rimmon and all the other Gods have conspired against me. Evil has come upon us. The priest, the King's High Priest has declared me a leper!

ZARA: A leper! Oh no, my Lord, wherefore . . .

MOTHER: (*rising, moves toward center*) The venemous liars! The evil creatures! May their throats be choked as they . . .

NAAMAN: Nay, mother, 'tis true. (*He pulls up his flowing sleeve to show his arm*) See . . . Mother . . . thy son is a leper! (*Naaman crosses Mother and moves toward divan.*)

MOTHER: A leper! The Gods forbid! The Captain of the King's hosts . . . a leper! (*She crosses Zara who stands center and then sits disconsolately on chair at right.*)

ZARA: (*moves toward Naaman at left of center and Hadassah moves down toward right chair to comfort mother*) My dear Lord . . . it must be something else . . . You cannot be a leper . . . you cannot! (*She sinks on floor near Naaman on divan.*)

NAAMAN: (*sadly*) Oh yes, my love! The Captain of the King's armies can destroy all his enemies and gather the treasures from all nations as spoil, but . . . no one can give him surety for his life. . . . (*He turns further away from Zara.*)

ZARA: (*rising and pacing up and down in center*) The Gods are jealous of my Lord's victories . . . that's it! Therefore they have smitten him. I know I should have given you my amulet! (*Suddenly, she remembers the King's magic necklace and moves toward Naaman at down left*) But, my Lord, what about the King's jewels that he gave you? Why did it not protect you?

NAAMAN: (*rising and crossing to up center as Zara crosses to left and downstage*) Strange, Zara, but I became a leper on the very day I put it on!

MOTHER: (*rising and crossing toward Naaman*) My son, make a great offering to the gods . . . sacrifice anything . . . everything. Surely, you can appease them.

NAAMAN: (*turning to face her*) It is impossible, Mother, for the priests have banished me from the temple. I cannot even speak to the gods.

ZARA: (*crosses to him as mother turns away toward divan*) But King Ben Hadad, Naaman . . . surely, he could command them to open the temple to you . . . (*She follows Naaman as he moves toward right.*)

NAAMAN: Dear little one, the King dare not defy the gods. Oh, yes! He will make a great offering for me and sacrifice a thousand oxen because he needs me. The tribes in the north have broken forth again . . . and are pouring into the villages of Lebanon. Yes, he needs me, but now, as a leper, my power is gone! I must live a prisoner in my own house. (*He moves far down right as he speaks.*) If I go into the highways, men will curse me; if I go to the market place, they will stone me. I tell you, the King's greatest Captain is cast into the dungeon of eternity!

HADASSAH: (*coming to Zara at center*) Cannot my Lord be happy in this beautiful house with my lovely Mistress?

ZARA: Nay, little maid. Men are not like us, content to stay in the home nest.

HADASSAH: But everything is so beautiful here!

NAAMAN: (*almost to himself at down right*) To rot to death piecemeal . . . a leper!

HADASSAH: (*horrified, again appeals to Zara*) But why does my Lord not go to the Prophet?

ZARA: To the Prophet? What Prophet, child?

HADASSAH: Is there not a Prophet in Damascus?

ZARA: (*shaking her head*) No, there is no Prophet here.

HADASSAH: But I don't understand! How can you . . . I mean, if my Lord were in my land, our Prophet could heal him of his leprosy.

ZARA: (*interested*) What's this you say, Hadassah? Your Prophet could heal him? (*Hadassah nods in agreement.*)

ZARA: (*approaching Naaman*) My Lord, do you hear what the child says? Hadassah, tell my Lord, tell him!

HADASSAH: (*to Naaman*) My Lord, Elisha, the Prophet that is in Samaria, I know he could cure you of your leprosy. If only you could come to my land!

NAAMAN: Nay, child . . . this is impossible!

MOTHER: (*rising and crossing a little toward center*) Not so, my son. Do travel to Samaria, and quickly!

NAAMAN: What? Chasing shadows? This is child's talk, Mother, some fairy tale. (*Hadassah wipes her tears away and looking hurt and worried, she retires upstage.*)

ZARA: My Lord, please! If you were bidden to do some great thing, would you not do it if promised a cure for your leprosy? It is just a small matter for you to travel to Samaria. Is it not worth it, my Lord, even if the healing were not found there?

NAAMAN: You are the light of my life, Zara, but alas, I cannot depart from my house!

MOTHER: Surely the King will send you if he is asked, son!

NAAMAN: I cannot petition the King, I cannot!

ZARA: Oh, my dear Lord, then let thy handmaid go to the King. I am but a woman; but they must admit the wife of the King's greatest Captain. I will take the child with me. Maybe we will find favor in his sight!

NAAMAN: I am ashamed to ask for such a childish thing. Men would point at me for a fool.

MOTHER: But they point at you now for a leper, son! Perhaps there is a chance that you will find a cure. Let them go, son, at once.

NAAMAN: (*after a pause*) Very well, then, go and do what you can. . . .

ZARA: Oh, thank you, my Lord! (*Hadassah echoes this remark*) We will go at once! (*As Naaman sits on chair at right, head in hands, the two women go off down left. Mother stands watching them leave us lights dim out and curtain falls.*)

* * * * * * * *

Scene 2

Before Elisha's house in Samaria. The Prophet is sitting before his door on a bench, reading from a tablet. His servant, Gehazi, enters through house door at left with a basin of water and towel.

GEHAZI: Your water, Master.

ELISHA: Thank you, Gehazi. You're a faithful servant indeed. (*There is a sound of rumbling of wheels off right.*)

ELISHA: What's that sound of heavy wheels? Did we expect a visitor at this hour?

GEHAZI: No, Master. (*He goes off to look left and quickly returns.*) It's a chariot at the gate, My Lord Elisha, in which rides a great Captain from Syria.

ELISHA: From Syria? What could he want of me?

GEHAZI: I'll go to greet him and inquire, Master. (*He exits at left.*)

ELISHA: (*praying aloud, lifting his eyes to Heaven and moving down left*) Great is your wisdom, my Heavenly Father. Please show me how I may help this stranger. Without you I can do naught! (*Gehazi enters from right. He is breathless and followed by Naaman's servant, carrying rich robes and jewels.*)

GEHAZI: My Lord Elisha, the Captain of the Syrian hosts begs for healing from his leprosy. He has sent these rich gifts to you — a thousand pieces of gold, five talents of silver, Syrian raiment and . . . (*Naaman's servant comes to center to present his gifts.*)

ELISHA: Nay, boy, take back the gold and silver to your master. See for yourself; (*he gestures*) have I not enough here? Sheep and oxen graze in my pastures and there is enough barley in the field to feed us all. Go, friend, depart in peace! Elisha does not serve or prophecy for rewards. I am only the humble servant of Jehovah, the God of Israel. Come, Gehazi, let us go in to supper. God speed you, friend. (*He bows, the servant bows, and he starts to leave at right. At this moment Naaman, impatient, enters and crosses to center.*)

NAAMAN: Where is this Prophet? Where is this Hebrew seer? Can he not come out to salute me? Why will he not take a gift from my hand? Is it not rich enough to suit his taste? Where is this prophet, I say — this prophet of a defeated nation?

ELISHA: (*hearing Naaman's voice, returns from his house to face Naaman at center*) Seekest thou Elisha, friend?

NAAMAN: Aye . . . that I do!

ELISHA: He is here before you, Sir. But he is not the Prophet of a defeated nation, but the Prophet of the God in Heaven in whose hands is every nation. All Kings shall fall down before Him. He alone can help you! (*Elisha exits into house at left.*)

NAAMAN: So this is the great Prophet!

NAAMAN'S SERVANT: Yes, Master. This is Elisha whom you seek.

NAAMAN: And he turns away. He will not even hear me. (*He crosses toward down right as Gehazi enters from house at left. He crosses to right of center.*)

GEHAZI: My Lord, Elisha asks the Syrian Captain if he will please drive to the Jordan River and there bathe himself seven times.

NAAMAN: What! To the Jordan! Am I a dog that he should turn his face from me, leave me standing here like some beggar? I thought he would wave his hand over the diseased place, call upon his God and the leprosy would depart. Instead, he tells me to go bathe in the

Jordan! Are not our Syrian rivers better than all the waters of Israel? Could I not wash in them and be clean? (*Gehazi bows and exits at left*) By the temple of Rimmon I shall tear his house down and burn it with fire! (*He paces about in a frenzy of anger.*)

NAAMAN's SERVANT: Nay, Master, not so fast! Harken, but a moment, I beseech you! (*He follows the angry Captain*) Perchance the Prophet does speak for some great God. If he had bidden thee do some great deed instead of bathing in the Jordan, wouldst thou not have done it?

NAAMAN: (*thoughtfully, and finally begrudgingly*) Perhaps. . . .

NAAMAN's SERVANT: Well, then? (*Gehazi appears in the doorway at left.*)

NAAMAN: Oh, very well . . . I suppose it can do no harm. . . . (*He turns to Gehazi*) Which way, I pray you, is this Jordan river?

GEHAZI: I will run before your chariot and direct your driver, Master. (*He exits at right and Naaman follows.*)

CURTAIN (OR BLACKOUT)

After a few moments—to represent the passage of hours—the lights come up and the curtain opens again. Elisha and Gehazi are watching off right.

GEHAZI: There it comes, my Lord, the chariot of the Syrian Captain.

ELISHA: Yes, he returns from the river. His walk is swift and joyful!

NAAMAN: (*as he enters at right*) Peace be to this house, Father. (*He bows.*)

ELISHA: And peace be to you, my son.

NAAMAN: (*almost beside himself with joy*) Behold now, behold me, Elisha! I am cleansed and made whole! I know now that there is no God in all the earth like the God of Israel. And you are indeed his Prophet. (*He bows again*) I washed myself seven times in the Jordan, as you directed and see (*He rolls up his sleeve*) my flesh is again like that of a little child. I pray you, Father, take some small present from your servant — ten talents of silver, a thousand gold pieces, it is such a little thing and you have given me back my life.

ELISHA: Nay, son, as Jehovah liveth, before whom I stand I can take nothing from thee!

NAAMAN: Not even some little thing, for thy great kindness to me?

ELISHA: I have done nothing, Naaman! Why should I receive? It is the hand of Jehovah that has touched thee and healed thee. Give thanks unto Him and bless His name. And do thou accept Jehovah's blessing . . . Jehovah who blesses thee and me and all His children on the earth.

NAAMAN: If you will not accept a gift, then give me now, I pray you, two mules' burden of earth to carry back to Damascus, that I may stand upon it every morning to pray to the God of Israel and give him thanks.

ELISHA: Surely thou mayest carry back Israel's soil to Damascus, if thou so desirest, but this is not necessary, my friend, for Jehovah is not the God of this land only, but of the whole world. Yes, the sea is his and he made it, the earth, and all that therein is!

NAAMAN: Then henceforth, even in the land of Rimmon, I shall worship no God but Jehovah, for he has given your servant life again. (*He kneels at Elisha's feet.*) Let me depart in peace, Father.

ELISHA: (*His hands lifted in blessing.*) Jehovah bless thee and keep thee . . . and may he make his face to shine upon thee and be gracious unto thee; may he lift up his countenance upon thee and give thee peace, now and forever!

(*The lights dim out on this picture of the conversion of the healed Naaman.*)

CURTAIN

MESSENGERS OF PEACE

A play based on the life of St. Paul

This play was born while my eighth grade church school class was involved with a detailed study of the life of the great missionary. The boys and girls of twelve and thirteen became extremely interested in the dramatic quality of this early Christian's boyhood, his intellectual curiosity, adventurous spirit and independent thinking. After several months of gathering material from novels and biographies as well as the New Testament, we decided to develop a five-scene play, based on critical moments in the life of this colorful man. The play presented here is really the work of a dozen or so boys and girls; their contributions and suggestions were invaluable. Although we did indulge in "poetic license" from time to time, for the sake of the drama, the plot line, for the most part, is based on factual material.

Characters

SAUL, as a boy, (the adult Paul)
BEN HANAN, his father
DEBORAH, Saul's mother
DAVID, a companion on the Damascus Road
SIMON, a second companion
SILAS, Paul's companion at Phillipi
MAGISTRATE of the court at Phillipi
JAILER, in Phillipi (the same actor can play the guard in the Roman prison)

AZEL, Saul's Grandfather
MIRIAM, his sister
GAMALIEL, the wise Rabbi teacher
THREE STUDENTS at Gamaliel's school
TIMOTHY, a Christian companion
LUKE, a doctor and Paul's good friend

Scene 1

The action takes place in Saul's home in Tarsus. His family are tentmakers, so a loom occupies a large part of stage left. A divan at right is the preferred seat for Grandfather Azel, a learned man, who, at curtain rise is reading the laws of his Fathers from parchment scrolls. Ben Hanan works at the loom from time to time. The door to the inner rooms is up left; the door to the outside is down right. At up center a long table for serving meals and several stone benches stand. At curtain rise Ben Hanan moves from the door at down right to his loom at left.

AZEL: No sign of the boy yet, son.

BEN H: No, Father.

AZEL: This is the third time in the last five days that Saul has not returned from school to study the Torah with me. I don't know what's come over the boy!

BEN H: I am troubled, too, Father. Strange things have happened to him lately. I know that something must be done, but what?

AZEL: He should be made to understand the importance of the great plans you have laid for him, Ben Hanan. Surely he knows that we have all hoped to see him become a great Rabbi one day, a teacher of his people! He must realize that if he does not study the Torah each day, he will never learn the laws of our Prophets.

BEN H: Yes, he knows, Father. He, too, hopes for that great day! He has told me so many times.

AZEL: I fear it is that Greek school that has changed him, Ben Hanan. Over and over I have warned you and Deborah that no good would come of allowing Saul to study with Nestor, and become friendly with these Greek and Roman boys.

BEN H: Perhaps you're right, Father; and yet you must admit that the lad has made great progress in his studies there. His master told me only yesterday, when he called at our shop to examine some tent cloth, that from the very beginning Saul has stood at the top of his class.

AZEL: (with cynicism) Yes . . . a class in wrestling, throwing the discus, and Greek philosophy! What good can possibly come of that, I ask you? A fine Hebrew boy, a Pharisee, spending hours of his time running races and going to the gymnasium. I tell you, son, it breaks my heart!

DEBORAH: (entering with Miriam from up left, carrying mats and plates of fruit) What? Saul not home yet?

BEN H: No sign of him, Deborah. Do you know where he could have gone, Miriam?

MIRIAM: No, Father. He said nothing to me of his plans.

AZEL: Deborah, you simply must talk to him. You can reason with the boy. This neglect of his duties here must be stopped. I think Saul will listen to you!

DEBORAH: (trying to protect Saul) Very well, I will speak to him, Father; but let us not be too hard on the boy. Perhaps he stopped in to see Ben Arza. He does sometimes, you know. He's so fond of the old Rabbi!

BEN H: Nay, Deborah, this time I feel that Father is right. Saul is old enough now to realize that if he is to learn a trade, and study to become a Rabbi one day, he cannot afford to waste these hours after he leaves the school.

SAUL: (*entering down right unobserved*) But he hasn't wasted them, Father. (*All turn at once in his direction; Deborah goes toward him at down right.*)

BEN H: Saul . . .

DEBORAH: My boy! I'm glad you've come at last! We were worried!

SAUL: I am sorry I was late again, Mother. (*He embraces her and crosses up to his grandfather*) And truly sorry that I missed my lesson, Grandfather. I just don't know where the time goes these days!

MIRIAM: (*genuinely hurt*) And you forgot all about our game, too, Saul. And you promised . . .

SAUL: (*crossing to Miriam*) No, Miriam, I didn't forget. But I just couldn't come today, I couldn't. (*Abashed, he crosses past her and to extreme left.*)

AZEL: Nor yesterday, nor the day before yesterday! It's always the same excuse, Saul! Well, today, you'd better have a better one!

SAUL: (*facing Azel*) Oh I have, Grandfather, I have. (*His eyes are shining*) The big grain ship from Alexandria docked today, and it was unloading this very afternoon. Joseph and I were helping, think of that! There were Assyrian magicians, and great casks of wine, and barrels of wheat and . . .

MIRIAM: Oh Saul, how exciting! (*She, too, is carried away by the adventure*) And did they really let you and Joseph go on the ship?

SAUL: (*still very excited*) Yes . . . yes! And then the Captain took us aboard the ship that stood next to his in the dock. It was filled with Roman soldiers!

DEBORAH: (*serious*) Soldiers! What are Roman soldiers doing here in Tarsus?

SAUL: They've come in the name of our Emperor, Mother, to protect the caravans from those robbers in the hills. You know the ones, Father . . . the ones that attacked Joseph's uncle's caravan.

BEN H: Why do you speak this way, Saul? You seem to have forgotten that you're a Jew, a Pharisee.

SAUL: No, I haven't Father; of course not. I haven't forgotten! I'm proud of belonging to the tribe of Benjamin, and I'm proud of the stripe on my robe that tells the whole world that I'm a Pharisee. But after all, we *are* Roman citizens, too.

MIRIAM: Yes, Father . . . Grandfather has told Saul and me many, many times about the great celebration here when Mark Antony came to Tarsus and . . .

SAUL: And how our family gave so much silver to help with the celebration that we received our citizenship in return.

BEN H: That is all true, Saul, but even though Rome governs us and the world, we must remember that we are different; our loyalties lie elsewhere. We are God's chosen people, Hebrews. It is our laws and our Prophets that we must study and obey. In these words only lies the truth!

AZEL: You have been too much with these Greek and Roman boys at Nestor's school, Saul. I tell you it is not healthy!

SAUL: But Grandfather, they are people just like ourselves; they think and feel, and love and hate, just as we do. It is interesting to find out why they believe as they do. I want to understand them, and maybe to help them. Is that so wrong?

DEBORAH: Surely the boy is right, Father. It can do no harm for him to learn about all people. It may be that one day he will be a teacher among the Greeks and Romans as well as the Hebrews.

SAUL: Yes, Grandfather, that's true. And there are so many things I must learn if I am really to prepare myself to teach. I want to understand why God created Jews and Gentiles and why they must remain so far apart. For a long time now, I have felt that . . . that . . . (*He is quiet and thoughtful now*) when our Messiah comes, he will come to all people, not as a Savior for the Jews alone but a Savior who will change the whole world. I only hope that I will see his coming!

BEN H: (*after a silent moment*) That is a worthy hope, my son . . . the hope of every single one of us! (*Saul seems to have cast a spell on the group. They are silent and thoughtful, deeply touched.*)

CURTAIN

Scene 2

Six years later, we find Saul in the Jerusalem school of Rabbi Gamaliel, the finest of all teachers of Jewish law. Azel and Ben Hanan have brought Saul to the Holy City to study with the renewed man. Here he has had a chance to read further the books of Plato and Aristotle, and the volumes of Roman law which enrich Gamaliel's extensive libraries. Saul has also heard, from his fellow students, about the carpenter from Galilee, who, because he called himself the

Messiah, was put to death as a false Prophet. This man's disciples, driven by his spirit, have gone about preaching his word; some have even dared to come into the temple at Jerusalem. Loyal and powerful Hebrews have determined that this lot, calling themselves Christians MUST be wiped out.

1st STUDENT: I tell you these disciples, as they call themselves, must be done away with.

2ND STUDENT: It is well that some of them have been imprisoned before they can do more harm!

3RD STUDENT: Yes, but if we're not careful, others will stir up riots in our Holy City, as they have elsewhere, preaching about this false Prophet, Jesus.

1st STUDENT: They're denying all of our Prophets' laws. . . .

SAUL: (*who has been listening as he paces back and forth upstage*) How could a Messiah, sent from God, come as a lowly carpenter? They are possessed of the devil, these disciples!

2ND STUDENT: They must be stoned, I say, as false teachers.

3RD STUDENT: Yes, for that is our law.

GAMALIEL: (*has entered unnoticed and heard the last two statements*) Wait, gentlemen! I say you must take care. I heard your plans for the followers of this Jesus. You must go slowly and consider well. It is my opinion that you had best let these men alone! If their council be the work of men, it will be overthrown; if it is of God, you cannot overthrow them, but, you can be accused of fighting against God.

SAUL: But, Master, they are deceiving the people! They must die . . . and Stephen, the leader, first of all.

1st STUDENT: They are dangerous to the faith, Master.

2ND STUDENT: Many of our people follow them and listen to their teaching.

GAMALIEL: Why do you wish to impose such a bloody sentence? Is it because they claim that this Jesus arose from the dead?

SAUL: No, Master, no! It is because they preach a false Messiah. Jesus is NOT the Messiah! If we set his disciples free, others will flock to their doctrine. As an example to the rest I vote that Stephen must die. . . .

GAMALIEL: (*turning sadly to the others*) And you?

ALL STUDENTS: Stone him, Master . . . Stephen must be stoned! (*They continue to cry for Stephen's death as the curtain falls.*)

CURTAIN

Scene 3

A place on the road to Damascus in the fiery heat of noon. Saul is on his way, with David and Simon, with orders from the Sanhedrin to destroy all the Christians they can find.

DAVID: We must be near Damascus now, Saul. I think I can make out the city walls yonder.

SAUL: That's good news, for I'm exhausted. The sun is beating down on us without mercy!

SIMON: Just as we shall beat down upon those followers of Jesus, wherever they are. Have you the High Priests' letters, David, giving us the authority to throw them all into prison?

DAVID: Indeed I have, Simon. (*He touches the leather pouch which hangs at his side*) I guard them with my life. (*He looks at Saul, who walks alone*) Saul, Master, you are brooding again. What is it? What is troubling you?

SAUL: I *am* troubled David! I feel very strange. I tell you, I have no more taste for our bloody errand.

SIMON: What? What are you saying?

DAVID: Surely you would not turn back now, Saul?

SIMON: Now that we have cleaned out the nest of heretics in Jerusalem, we must wipe out their new center in Damascus.

SAUL: (*still troubled*) Yes . . . yes . . . I know, I know. . . . But Stephen's eyes are haunting me I tell you!

DAVID: Stephen, you said?

SIMON: Yes, he that we stoned to death by the city gate.

DAVID: Oh, yes, I remember! Clever old man, but misled. Too bad!

SAUL: Misled or not, he haunts me day after day. I can see his eyes lifted up to Heaven as he said, "Lord Jesus, receive my spirit, lay not this sin to their charge." What is it that can make a man die like that? Whence comes such courage?

SIMON: He was just keeping face, that's all.

DAVID: He was afraid, all right, Saul. He was just too proud to show it.

SAUL: No, you're wrong, both of you. Cowards curse, but Stephen prayed to this Jesus whose followers we are trying to destroy.

SIMON: Nonsense, Brother Saul. You're tired. You'll see more clearly when we reach Damascus.

DAVID: Rest here, Saul, while we fetch water from the stream yonder. (*They exit and Saul stands motionless, as if in a trance. Suddenly strange, ethereal music is heard and a white beam of light falls directly on Saul's face. He is blinded by its intensity.)*

VOICE: (*off*) Saul! Saul! Why persecutest thou me?

SAUL: (*kneeling, looking up into the light*) Who . . . who art thou, Lord?

VOICE. (*off*) I am Jesus, whom thou persecutest. Arise, Saul and stand upon your feet. (*Saul obeys*) I have appeared unto you to appoint you my minister and witness. Go forth to open the eyes of the Gentiles that they may turn from darkness to light, and live the way of life I came to teach.

SAUL: I, Lord? I, Saul of Tarsus?

VOICE: (*off*) Even so! And from this time forward you shall be called Paul.

SAUL: Yes, Lord Jesus! I hear your words and I shall obey! (*Music builds to a climax as Saul falls on his knees, looking up into the light which gradually dims to black out.)*

CURTAIN

Scene 4

The prison at Phillippi, several years and two missionary journeys later. Paul and Silas, arrested for their preaching in the city, have been taken before the Roman Magistrate, flogged, and imprisoned.

PAUL: Even though we are behind bars once again, Silas, I am glad that we came to Macedonia.

SILAS: Yes, I too, brother, only last night Lydia's whole family, even the servants, asked if they might become Christians.

PAUL: Our little company grows stronger every day, friend.

SILAS: (*listening*) Wait! I hear footsteps. The Jailer must be bringing us the guest he promised.

PAUL: Fear not, Silas. God has his plan for us . . . we must trust him.

MAGISTRATE. (*entering with Jailer*) See here, you Jews, I want to make sure that you understand the seriousness of your offense. You have been disturbing the whole city, preaching about this new way of life. You are tempting our citizens to idleness and heresy. . . .

PAUL: Your Honor, we ARE Jews, as you have said, and we serve Jesus, the Christ. We bring no trouble or harm to your people, only new understanding of the power of love.

MAGISTRATE: I say you are trouble-makers, both of you, and I order you to be silent in the future. (*To Jailer:*) Beat them again tomorrow, Jailer, and if they should escape, I'll have your head. . . .

SILAS: But, Your Honor, my friend is ill, and besides he is a Roman citizen and he has the right to . . .

MAGISTRATE: No matter, we have no time to listen to your prattle. And you, Jailer, you'd best remember my words. Do you understand?

JAILER: (*as he shows Magistrate out*) Oh yes, Sire, yes. . . .

PAUL: (*finally breaking the silence*) God has his own reason for all of this, you may be sure, Silas.

SILAS: Yes, brother, I must believe that. (*After a short pause, the distant sounds of an earthquake's thunderous rumbling begin*) What strange sounds are those? There is a rumbling beneath our feet!

PAUL: (*swaying unsteadily*) There is a sound of crumbling stone. An earthquake, Silas. It is an earthquake!

SILAS: See . . . the locks have fallen from the doors! They stand wide open! (*Lights go off as he moves to look off into the hallway*) The other prisoners are all in flight, brother!

JAILER: (*calling offstage*) A light! A light, I say. Give me a light! (*He enters carrying torch*) Jews, where are you? I tell you, if you have escaped with the rest, I am . . .

PAUL: (*approaching him to take his hand*) Fear not, friend! We are still here.

JAILER: (*amazed*) But why? Had you no legs to run like the others?

PAUL: Yes, of course. But if we had escaped, you might suffer death tomorrow. Remember the Magistrate's threat? We could not risk your life, man; that Christ would not have us do; that he would never do. So . . . you see . . . we remain!

JAILER: (*incredulous*) You mean . . . you mean . . . you stayed here to save me? But I beat you only today. And you stayed because of this Christ you worship?

SILAS: Yes . . . because of him.

JAILER: (*pauses, deep in thought*) Will you, will you come to my house tonight, friends, and tell me about him you worship. I think that I, too, would be a follower of this Christ, if I could understand.

PAUL: That we will, my friend, and gladly.

SILAS: Lead the way. . . . (*They start to go off stage following the Jailer.*)

CURTAIN

Scene 5

Paul's cell in the Roman prison. He is nearly sixty now, and has grown weary and steadily weaker from the pressures of his missionary travels. He has been given the death sentence.

LUKE: Courage, Brother Paul. It is yet an hour until dawn. Timothy may yet be here!

PAUL: It is strange, my longing to die in my old cloak and to have my scrolls and records here. I suppose I want them near me because they contain the names of all those who have believed in Christ through our preaching. I call them my "book of life." Luke!

LUKE: (*at barred window*) Brother, I think I hear horses' hoofs in the street below. . . . It must be Timothy. Thank God he has come!

PAUL: Amen!

TIMOTHY: (*entering and going to embrace Paul*) My dear brother Paul! Luke!

PAUL: Timothy, my son in Christ, you have come in time . . . in time!

TIMOTHY: Yes, I am here at last, dear brother and I brought your cloak and the scrolls as you requested. (*He gives them to Paul.*)

PAUL: (*lovingly fingering his cloak*) This is the cloak I made of tent-cloth when I was in Corinth with Aquila and Priscilla. It will protect me from the mists of the morning on the Ostian Way.

TIMOTHY: Why are you going out so early, Paul? Surely you are not well enough just now.

PAUL: (*after an awkward silence, approaches Timothy*) My son, I have not told you . . . but . . . this very morning, I must die. The second trial went against me. I am condemned as a trouble-maker.

TIMOTHY: What! You, who have brought peace and love to everyone, everywhere . . . ?

PAUL: No matter! For me, to live is Christ and to die is gain.

LUKE: Sit down, Paul, and rest. The soldiers will be here soon.

PAUL: Yes! (*He sits quietly*) Let me look once more into my book of life. (*He looks at his scrolls*) Here they are, those dear names — Barnabas, Silas, Timothy, Luke, my fellow workers — and all those cities we have visited, Antioch . . . all those in Galatia . . . Troas, where I saw the vision . . . Phillippi, where we had the earthquake. Yes . . . and then Athens, Corinth and Ephesus. At the end I must write Rome, for the very soldiers who guard me here believe now! (*He writes.*)

TIMOTHY: (*listening, moves toward Paul and touches his shoulder*) Brother . . . they are coming.

PAUL: (*closes the scroll as the steps grow louder*) Yes, the hour is at hand! Let us pray together before we go to meet them. (*The three bow their heads*) Gladly I come to Thee, my Father. I have fought the good fight; I have finished the course; I have kept the faith! (*The door is opened and the light from the Soldiers' torches floods the room. Paul in his cloak, followed by Luke and Timothy, who carries the scrolls, walk bravely into the light. The curtain closes on the empty cell and one hears the marching footsteps fading in the distance.*)

CURTAIN

8

In Conclusion

As I approach this final chapter, several questions come to mind. Why did I feel so compelled to get these thoughts on paper? Have I achieved my stated objectives? Are the arguments for creative drama, as a force in furthering Christian behavior, convincing?

You, the reader, and only you, can respond with any certainty to some of the queries. By attempting to answer some of the others, I can, perhaps, tie some of the loose threads together, thereby wrapping up the meaning of the total package.

WHY DID I FEEL COMPELLED TO GET THESE THOUGHTS ON PAPER?

A careful and troubled look at young people in today's world was the first motivation. A thoughtful, sympathetic analysis of some Church school teachers and youth workers was the second. As Rollo May said in a recent lecture at Johns Hopkins University, " . . . we are living in a psychotic age where advanced technology runs our lives for us. We are suffering from anxieties caused by the breakdown in our trust and world-shaking events like the tragic war in Vietnam." He firmly believes that what we have created controls us and our behavior. Survival, in such a period, depends upon the commitment and spirit of those who use technology. He further implies, and I agree, that we feel helpless and small as individuals. Too often we submit to an inescapable levelling force, almost living a prologue to Orwell's *1984*.

Neither children nor adults have yet become the robot-like creatures Orwell describes; nonetheless, some of their characteristics are alarmingly evident. All about us we note cold indifference, uniformity, lack of humanity, compassion, or faith; there is little caring, sensitivity or responsiveness. Results of this point of view are obvious: cynicism, black humor, lack of inner discipline, amorality, greed, a frightening isolationism and a self-centered, "do-your-own-thing" philosophy. These are patently not the attributes of the Christian personality. The patterns of behavior bequeathed to us by our forebears, seem to have fallen by the wayside, "unwept, unhonored and unsung." People are frantically searching for support, security, direction, for a WAY! This is exemplified by the sudden interest in the mystical eastern cultures. The increasing following of such religious cults as the Hari Krishna group testifies to this trend.

As Church school teachers, we must recognize our responsibility and privilege to provide a *way* . . . and to motivate healthy growth and change in our young people. We must endeavor to help them to understand, honor, and practice basic Christian principles, and by their examples, carry the *Good News* to all who cross their path. It has been said, many times, that a society is only as great as the spirit of each individual within it. We, then, through encouraging each child to a fuller realization of his own potential and a deep love for and understanding of his fellow man, are contributing to the building of a better world. Most psychologists agree that acceptance of, or *love* of, one's self and others is fundamental to the constructive, joyous, fulfilling life of the individual. He who feels insecure and inadequate expresses hostility toward others; they, in turn, seem to reject him and the more he tries in awkward ways to make himself acceptable, the more he fails. The targets of his hostility increase to include his destiny, the world, and eventually himself. His whole state of being is negative and destructive.

This attitude is the direct antithesis of self-realization which, according to Paul Tillich can only occur " . . . when the NEW BEING appears . . . when one feels united with God, the ground and the meaning of one's existence. . . . Then one has the astonishing experience of feeling reunited with one's self, in deep self-acceptance. One accepts one's self as something which is eternally important, eternally loved and eternally accepted." And he goes on to say that: " . . . joy is not merely fleeting temporal happiness, but the expression of essential fulfillment . . . joy is nothing else than the awareness of our being filled in our own true being, possible only when we unite ourselves with others as we really are."

We should not be discouraged if, despite our best efforts, the emergence of the real self seems to take an eternity. We must realize that it is a continuous journey; one never really arrives — he is forever arriving. This is the real art of education, to nourish and to cause to grow, as someone has so aptly said. To find the "stuff" of nourishment, new enriching experiences, ways of deepening awareness and sensitivity is our task. It is my firm belief that a continuing utilization of creative drama techniques can facilitate this work. As a child is gradually able to interact imaginatively with his peers, express his thoughts and feelings freely, he begins to establish a new self-confidence. Because he is comfortable with himself, he can afford to be open and responsive to those about him, to deepen his relationships and develop his compassion.

Skillfully selected dramatic situations, in which the Christian point of view is implicit, can involve a world of human relationships. Through sincere discussion and playing out of such material, the participant absorbs invaluable knowledge of sound Christian behavior patterns, which subconsciously become an intrinsic part of his living philosophy. It is a long acknowledged fact that conditioning, not intellectual learning, cultivates attitudes. In improvisation, one experiences vicariously many real life situations and is motivated by the deep human emotions of others in conflict and crises. He finds himself reacting consistently and naturally to solve these problems and, in the process, he widens his knowledge of sound behavior principles.

As early as the fourteenth century, God-fearing men were expressing the same convictions. The following lines from a sermon given in an English church in the mid-thirteen hundreds defend the idea of presenting Miracle Plays in the church. " . . . profitable to men and to the worship of God it is to seeken all the means by which men may see sin and drawen them to virtues . . . now it is timely and skilful to assayen to converten the people by plays and games, as by miracle-playing . . . since it is lawful to have the miracles of God painted, why is it not as well lawful to have the miracles of God played, since men may better readen the will of God and His marvellous works in the playing of them than in the painting? . . . and better they be holden in men's minds . . . by the playing of them than by the painting, for this is a dead book, the other a quick."

CAN THE STEP-BY-STEP METHOD PROVE HELPFUL?

I reply to my own question with an unequivocal affirmative. You will find evidence to reinforce my firm conviction if you will recall, for a moment, the natural steps in the growth and development of a human being. The baby moves his arms, legs and body before he can stand or speak; he crawls before he can walk; he uses a few words as he moves about with assistance; finally, he can both walk and talk independently. The procedures for the creative dramatics project recommended in this book follow the same natural pattern. First, activity pantomime or simple movement; then more complex movement motivated by one mood; and then by several moods. When this is achieved, you begin to use a word or a phrase, and, at long last, a whole scene is played in improvised dialogue. The method is almost foolproof! But any effort to hurry things and put "the cart before the horse" may meet with dismal failure.

Since these techniques were developed during many years of experimentation and have proved unusually successful, I cannot urge too strongly that they be adopted by the religious education teacher or group leader. The spontaneous enthusiasm of the children participating as they gradually sense, with great pleasure, their growing inner selves, is the best evidence of the success of the project. This joy exists only when the choice of material and rate of progress is appropriate. Children's response is a trusty barometer!

Finally, let me suggest that we be guided by the wisdom of hundreds of educators, philosophers and psychologists. Most of them are well aware of the fundamental human need for creative expression, some activity through which one can find emotional release and stimulation of the imagination. The remarkable power of drama as the preferred activity is so perfectly stated by Dr. Harold Ehrensperger in his book that I feel he must have the last words in mine:

"It is only as one makes the effort to better the state of mankind that he becomes the mature person with vision, the integrated personality." Such a process, Ehrensperger insists, requires imagination and it is the dramatic instinct that especially calls forth imaginative faculties "by enabling the person to put himself in someone else's place. If we are to be persons who are sensitive to other men, if we are to relate ourselves to God, we must have the capacity to imagine."

These treasured thoughts should leave no doubt in the mind of the conscientious, idealistic teacher as to what direction he must take. If his work in creative drama can help to build sensitive, integrated personalities who may eventually share in bringing about a renaissance of the life of the spirit on earth, has he really any alternative?

LIST OF RESOURCES

BOOKS AND ARTICLES ON CREATIVE DRAMATICS

ALLSTROM, ELIZABETH. *You Can Teach Creatively.* New York: The Abingdon Press, 1970.

ANDERSON, BARBARA. "Creative Dramatics: A Good Way to Teach." *International Journal of Religious Education* (October, 1956), pp. 8, 9, 48.

BURGER, ISABEL B. *Creative Play Acting,* 2nd rev. ed. New York: The Ronald Press Co., 1966.

CITRON, SAMUEL J. *Dramatics for Creative Teaching.* New York: United Synagogue Commission on Jewish Education, 1961.

DURLAND, FRANCES C. *Creative Dramatics for Children: A Practical Manual for Teachers and Leaders.* Kent, Ohio: Kent State University Press, 1975.

FITZGERALD, BURDETTE. *Let's Act the Story.* San Francisco: Fearen Publishing Co., 1957.

HARDY, SISTER MARIA PAULA. "Drama as a Tool in Education." Unpublished Ph.D. dissertation, University of Illinois, 1972.

HARTLEY, RUTH E., LAWRENCE, F. and GOLDENSON, R. *Understanding Children's Play.* New York: Columbia University Press, 1952.

HEINIG, RUTH B. and STILLWELL, LYDIA. *Creative Dramatics for the Classroom Teacher.* Englewood Cliffs, N.J.: Prentice-Hall, Inc., 1974.

McCASLIN, NELLIE. *Creative Dramatics in the Classroom.* 2nd ed. New York: David McKay Co. Inc., 1974.

McINTYRE, BARBARA. *Informal Dramatics: A Language Arts Activity for the Special Pupil.* Pittsburgh: Stanwix House, Inc., 1963.

MORRISON, E. S. and FOSTER, V. E. "The Use of Creative Drama with Children." *International Journal of Religious Education* (September, 1963), pp. 6-9.

PEMBERTON-BILLING, R. N. and CLEGG, J. B. *Teaching Drama.* London: University of London Press, 1966.

SCHWARTZ, D. T. and ALDRICH D. *Give Them Roots and Wings.* Washington, D.C.: American Theatre Association, 1972.

SIKS, GERALDINE B. *Creative Dramatics, an Art for Children.* New York: Harper and Row, 1958.

Siks, G. and Dunnington, H. *Children's Theatre & Creative Dramatics.* Seattle: University of Washington Press, 1961.

Ward, Winifred. *Playmaking with Children.* New York: Appleton-Century-Crofts, 1957.

Warge, Dan and Dorothy. *Dramatics in the Christian School.* St. Louis: Concordia Publishing House, 1966.

Woody, Pam. "Creative Dramatics with Preschool Children in a Religious Education Program." Unpublished paper, California State University, 1975.

BOOKS USEFUL FOR GENERAL BACKGROUND AND APPRECIATION

Chaplin, Dora. *Children and Religion.* New York: Charles Scribner's Sons, 1961.

Cole, Natalie. *Arts in the Classroom.* New York: John Day, 1940.

Courtney, Richard. *Play, Drama and Thought.* London & Worcester: The Trinity Press, 1974.

Dixon, Madeleine. *High, Wide and Deep.* New York: John Day, 1947.

Ehrensperger, Harold. *Religious Drama, Ends and Means.* New York: Abingdon Press, 1962.

Huizinga, Johan. *Homo Ludens: A Study of the Play Element in Culture.* Boston: The Beacon Press, 1955.

Jones, Robert Edmond. *The Dramatic Imagination.* New York: Theatre Arts Books, 1941.

Mearns, Hughes. *Creative Power: The Education of Youth in the Creative Arts.* New York: Dover Publications, Inc., 1958.

Mosely, J. E. *Using Drama in the Church.* rev. ed. St. Louis: Bethany Press, 1962.

Selden, Samuel. *Man in His Theatre.* Chapel Hill, N.C.: University of North Carolina Press, 1957.

Shaftel, F. and G. *Role-Playing for Social Values.* Englewood Cliffs, N.J.: Prentice-Hall Inc., 1967.

Stanislavsky, C. *My Life in Art.* New York: Theatre Arts Books.

Wieman, Regina W. *The Family Lives its Religion.* New York: Harper & Brothers, 1941.

MATERIALS FOR STORY PLAYING AND IMPROVISATION

Allstrom, Elizabeth. *Let's Play a Story.* New York: The Friendship Press, 1957.

ARBUTHNOT, M. H. *The Arbuthnot Anthology of Children's Literature.* 4th ed. New York: Scott, Foresman & Co., 1976.

KASE, ROBERT. *Stories for Creative Acting.* New York: Samuel French, Inc., 1961.

SIKS, GERALDINE B. *Children's Literature for Dramatization.* New York: Harper and Row, 1964.

TAYLOR, LOREN E. *Storytelling and Dramatization.* Minneapolis: Burgess Publishing Co., 1965.

WARD, WINIFRED. *Stories to Dramatize.* Anchorage, Ky.: The Anchorage Press, 1952.

PRODUCTION, DIRECTING AND GENERAL TECHNICAL INFORMATION

ADIX, VERN. *Theatre Scenecraft.* Anchorage, Ky.: The Anchorage Press, 1957.

BARTON, LUCY. *Historic Costume for the Stage.* rev. ed. Boston: Baker's Plays, 1961.

BURRIS-MEYER, H. and COLE, EDWARD C. *Scenery for the Theatre.* 2nd rev. ed. Boston: Little Brown, 1972.

CORNBERG, SOL and GEBAUER, EMANUEL. *A Stage Crew Handbook.* rev. ed. New York: Harper and Row, 1957.

CORSEN, RICHARD. *Stage Make-Up.* 5th ed. Englewood Cliffs, N.J.: Prentice-Hall, Inc., 1974.

DAVIS, J. and WATKINS, M. J. *Children's Theatre.* New York: Harper and Row, 1960.

DEAN, ALEXANDER and CARRA, L. *Fundamentals of Play Directing.* 3rd ed. New York: Holt, Rinehart and Winston, 1974.

GASSNER, JOHN and BARBER, P. *Producing the Play.* rev. ed. Bd. with *New Scene Technician's Handbook.* New York: Holt, Rinehart and Winston, 1953.

SELDON, SAMUEL. *First Steps in Acting.* 2nd ed. New York: Irvington Publishers, Inc., 1964.

SELDEN, S. and SELLMAN H. D. *Stage Scenery and Lighting.* 3rd ed. New York: Appleton-Century-Crofts, 1959.

WARD, WINIFRED. *Theatre for Children.* Anchorage, Ky.: The Anchorage Press, 1958.